Praise for *Th[e Whale]*

"Beautifully devastating . . . *The Whale* manages to be about so very much at once: writing, parenting, teaching, religion, body image, overeating, the price paid by gay couples born in the wrong state or just a few years too soon. But, most of all, *The Whale* is a remarkably eloquent exploration of the way the need for honesty overwhelms us when we sense that our time is short."

—Chris Jones, *Chicago Tribune*

"A vibrant, provocative new play . . . The sharp-eared skill and sensitivity with which Hunter explores his thickly layered material are matched by his fair-mindedness."

—Michael Feingold, *Village Voice*

"Extraordinary . . . Hunter has constructed an outsize, gothic scenario in tender miniature, against a backdrop so blandly bleak we brace ourselves for despair: the sound of cascading highway traffic braids itself with the crashing surf inside Charlie's head. Is it all just too much? Never for a second."

—Scott Brown, *New York*

"A deeply affecting and piercingly amusing play about guilt and connection . . . Hunter has given all of these funny-sad lost souls details that emerge bit by bit and twist and expand the story in compelling ways."

—Joe Dziemianowicz, *New York Daily News*

"*The Whale* is tragedy in a minor key, about a man torn between flesh and spirit . . . Humane, sharp and often funny."

—David Cote, *TimeOut New York*

"Samuel D. Hunter's compelling, psychologically complex play takes the audience to the confounding no man's land of nihilism."

—John Lahr, *New Yorker*

Praise for *A Bright New Boise*

"A dark, droll and ultimately explosive work . . . Funny, compassionate and disturbing all at once, Hunter's quintessentially American scenario portrays an individual trapped in an emotional and cultural wasteland, his life configured by uncaring impersonal forces, his spirit hobbled by unnamed guilt."

—Deborah Klugman, *LA Weekly*

"A simple, superb little heartland heartbreaker . . . This is a rube tragedy—a respectful and honest-feeling one, for a change, with unquenchable humor and scrupulous emotional honesty—and by jingo, it sings."

—Scott Brown, *New York*

"Exhilarating . . . *A Bright New Boise* is an unsparing account of the hunger pangs in the barren American gut . . . Hunter has such highly sensitive antennae for the look and rhythm of mundane places that *A Bright New Boise* develops an authentic texture, separate from other pieces in its genre."

—Peter Marks, *Washington Post*

"Despite the crisp wind of despair that blows all through Samuel D. Hunter's beautifully realized *A Bright New Boise*, this clear-eyed comedy about faith's meager harvest will still lift your heart. Some of it is simple delight in craft . . . The rest of our pleasures lie in Hunter's gentle characterizations, a plot that mingles absurdity and genuine philosophical investigation."

—Helen Shaw, *TimeOut New York*

"An anxious, funny look at the messianic and the mundane in America . . . Hunter delivers these characters and their crucibles with tenderness and rage. For all its mistrust of religion, the play is a kind of prayer."

—Charlotte Stoudt, *Los Angeles Times*

The Whale

A Bright New Boise

The Whale

A Bright New Boise

Samuel D. Hunter

THEATRE COMMUNICATIONS GROUP
NEW YORK
2014

The publication of *The Whale* and *A Bright New Boise*, by Samuel D. Hunter,
through TCG's Book Program, is made possible in part by the New York
State Council on the Arts with the support of Governor Andrew Cuomo and
the New York State Legislature.

TCG books are exclusively distributed to the book trade by Consortium Book
Sales and Distribution.

LIBRARY OF CONGRESS CATALOGING-IN-PUBLICATION DATA
Hunter, Samuel D.
[Plays. Selections]
The whale / A bright new boise / Samuel D. Hunter.
pages cm
ISBN 978-1-55936-460-7 (paperback)
ISBN 978-1-55936-776-9 (ebook)
I. Title. II. Title: Bright new boise.
PS3608.U59496A6   2014
812'.6—dc23   2014019190

Book design and composition by Lisa Govan
Cover design by Rodrigo Corral Design / Rachel Adam Rogers

First Edition, August 2014
Second Printing, January 2023

For Davis,
without whom these plays
would not have been realized;
and
For John,
without whom
these plays would not exist

———————

Contents

The Whale

PRODUCTION HISTORY

The Whale was developed with support of PlayPenn (Paul Meshejian, Artistic Director) and, in part, at the Icicle Creek Theatre Festival (Allen Fitzpatrick, Artistic Director). It was awarded the 2011 Sky Cooper New American Play Prize at Marin Theatre Company (Jasson Minadakis, Artistic Director; Ryan Rilette, Producing Director).

The Whale received its world premiere at the Denver Center Theatre Company (Kent Thompson, Artistic Director; Charles Varin, Managing Director) on January 13, 2012. The production was part of the Colorado New Play Summit and was directed by Hal Brooks. The set design was by Jason Simms, the costume design was by Kevin Copenhaver, the lighting design was by Seth Reiser and the sound design was by William Burns; the production stage manager was A. Phoebe Sacks. The cast was:

CHARLIE	Tom Alan Robbins
LIZ	Angela Reed
ELDER THOMAS	Cory Michael Smith
ELLIE	Nicole Rodenburg
MARY	Tasha Lawrence

The Whale opened at Playwrights Horizons (Tim Sanford, Artistic Director; Leslie Marcus, Managing Director; Carol Fishman, General Manager) in New York City, on November 5, 2012. The production was directed by Davis McCallum. The set design was by Mimi Lien, the costume design was by Jessica Pabst, the lighting design was by Jane Cox and the sound design was by Fitz Patton; the production stage manager was Alaina Taylor. The cast was:

CHARLIE	Shuler Hensley
LIZ	Cassie Beck/Rebecca Henderson
ELDER THOMAS	Cory Michael Smith
ELLIE	Reyna de Courcy
MARY	Tasha Lawrence

The play opened at South Coast Repertory (Marc Masterson, Artistic Director; Paula Tomei, Managing Director) in Costa Mesa, California, on March 15, 2013. The production was directed by Martin Benson. The set design was by Thomas Buderwitz, the costume design was by Angela Balogh Calin, the lighting design was by Donna and Tom Ruzika, and the original music and sound design were by Michael Roth; the production stage manager was Jennifer Ellen Butler. The cast was:

CHARLIE	Matthew Arkin
LIZ	Blake Lindsley
ELDER THOMAS	Wyatt Fenner
ELLIE	Helen Sadler
MARY	Jennifer Christopher

The play opened at Victory Gardens Theater (Chay Yew, Artistic Director; Chris Mannelli, Interim Managing Director) in Chicago, Illinois, on April 15, 2013. The production was directed by Joanie Schultz. The set design was by Chelsea Warren, the costume design was by Janice Pytel, the lighting design was by Heather Gilbert and the sound design was by Thomas Dixon; the production stage manager was Tina M. Jach. The cast was:

CHARLIE	Dale Calandra
LIZ	Cheryl Graeff
ELDER THOMAS	Will Allan
ELLIE	Leah Karpel
MARY	Patricia Kane

Characters

CHARLIE	Male, weighing around six hundred pounds, early to mid-forties
LIZ	Female, mid to late thirties
ELDER THOMAS	Male, nineteen
ELLIE	Female, seventeen
MARY	Female, early to mid-forties

Setting

Northern Idaho, the present.

The main room of a small, white-walled, desolate apartment in a cheaply constructed two-story building. The room is dominated by a large couch that sags in the middle, reenforced by several cinder blocks.

Within arm's reach of the couch are a small computer desk on rollers with a laptop, a large pile of papers, a claw for reaching, and a whole universe of full, empty and half-empty food containers (doughnuts, candy bars, fried chicken, burgers, two-liter soda bottles, etc.). A walker rests near the couch somewhere. An aging TV sits in a corner. Little effort has been made to clean up trash or organize.

A small kitchen is off to one corner of the stage; a bathroom and bedroom offstage.

Notes

The play is served much better by being performed without an intermission (running time is roughly one hour, fifty minutes). However, if absolutely necessary, an intermission can be taken in between Wednesday night and Thursday morning.

Dialogue written in *italics* is emphatic, deliberate; dialogue written in ALL CAPS is impulsive, explosive.

A " / " indicates an overlap in dialogue.

Monday

MORNING

Charlie, dressed in oversized sweatpants and an oversized sweat-shirt, sits on the couch, speaking into a small microphone hooked up to a laptop.

CHARLIE: This is from a paper I got from a student last year, a freshman at UC Santa Barbara. He was writing this for an American Lit class. It's a paper about *The Great Gatsby*.

(Pulling out an essay) "There were many aspects to the book *The Great Gatsby*. But I was bored by it because it was about people that I don't care about and they do things I don't understand. In conclusion, *The Great Gatsby* wasn't so great, LOL." *(Stops reading)*

The problems with this essay are painfully obvious. The student has no discernible thesis, almost no analysis whatsoever . . . I'll be posting the paper in its entirety, what I want you to do is read through it a few times, and then post a three- to four-paragraph response providing concrete ideas for revision. Also, those of you who haven't given me paper four, I need it by five o'clock, *no exceptions.* And remember—the more revision you guys do on these papers, the better. The more you can change, chances are the stronger these papers will be. All right?

AFTERNOON

Charlie, in the same position as before, in front of his laptop, mastur-bating to gay porn.

After a few moments, his breathing becomes more and more shallow. He pushes the computer desk away from him. He feels some sharp pain in his chest.

He reaches toward his cell phone, but accidentally knocks it onto the floor. The pain becomes worse. All the while, the gay porn is still playing in the background.

Charlie takes some deep breaths, wheezing loudly, trying to calm himself down.

A knock at the door.

CHARLIE: Liz?!

(Another knock.)

It's not locked, just come in! I need help, I—!

(Elder Thomas enters, wearing a white shirt, black tie, and black slacks. He holds some books and a bike helmet.)

ELDER THOMAS: Oh, my God. Oh, Gosh, are you—? *(Pause)* I should call an ambulance. Should I call an ambulance?

(Elder Thomas notices the gay porn, still playing. Charlie quickly reaches over and shuts his laptop.)

I don't have a phone, do you have—?

(Charlie pulls out a few sheets of paper, hands them to Elder Thomas.)

CHARLIE: Read this to me.

ELDER THOMAS: Wait, what?

CHARLIE: Read it to me, *please*.

ELDER THOMAS: I have to call you an ambulance! I don't know what to do, I'm just—

CHARLIE: I don't know what's going to happen in the next five minutes. Please, read it to me. PLEASE JUST READ IT TO ME.

ELDER THOMAS: OKAY! OKAY, I JUST—

(Reading, quickly) "In the amazing book *Moby Dick* by the author Herman Melville, the author recounts his story of being at sea. In the first part of his book, the author, calling himself Ishmael, is in a small seaside town and he is sharing a bed with a man named Queequeg—" *(Stops)*

What is this?! Why am I reading this?! I need to call someone!—

CHARLIE *(Pleading)*: PLEASE JUST READ IT. *ANY OF IT.*

ELDER THOMAS *(Reading)*: "I was very saddened by this book, and I felt many emotions for the characters. And I felt saddest of all when I read the boring chapters that were only descriptions of whales, because I knew that the author was just trying to save us from his own sad story, just for a little while. This book made me think about my own life, and then it . . . It made me feel . . ."

(Charlie's breathing starts to become normal. He takes a few deep breaths, calming himself down.)

Did that—help?

CHARLIE: Yes. Yes, it did.

ELDER THOMAS: I'm calling an ambulance, where's your phone?

CHARLIE: I don't go to hospitals.

ELDER THOMAS: I can't help you, I don't even know CPR!—

CHARLIE: *I don't go to hospitals. (Pause)* I'm sorry. Excuse me, I'm sorry. You can go if you want, I . . . Thank you for reading that to me.

(Pause. Elder Thomas doesn't move.)

ELDER THOMAS: Are you feeling better?

CHARLIE: Yes.

ELDER THOMAS: Are you sure?

CHARLIE: Yes.

ELDER THOMAS: Okay. Um. I— *(Pause)* I represent the Church of Jesus Christ of Latter Day Saints? We're sharing a message for all faiths?

CHARLIE: Oh.

ELDER THOMAS: Yeah. *(Pause)* Would you—like to hear about the church?

(Pause.)

CHARLIE: Okay.

ELDER THOMAS: Really?

CHARLIE: Yes. Actually, yes. *(Pause)* But I should call my friend. My friend is a nurse. She should come over. She knows what to do, she—takes care of me.

ELDER THOMAS: Okay, good, where's your—?
CHARLIE: My cell phone is over there, can you get it for me?

(Charlie points to his cell phone. Elder Thomas picks up the cell phone and hands it to Charlie.)

ELDER THOMAS: Do you want me to— . . . ?
CHARLIE: Stay with me.

(Pause.)

ELDER THOMAS: I really should—
CHARLIE: I'm not sure what's going to happen right now. I'd—
 rather there was someone here with me. If that's all right.
ELDER THOMAS: Yeah, okay.
CHARLIE: Thank you.

(Pause.)

ELDER THOMAS: What was—? That thing I read to you about
 Moby Dick?
CHARLIE: It was an essay. It's my job, I do online tutoring,
 online classes on expository writing.
ELDER THOMAS: But why did you want me to read that to you?
CHARLIE: Because I thought I was dying. And I wanted to hear
 it one last time.

LATER THAT AFTERNOON

Charlie sits on the couch, Liz stands over him, taking his blood pressure. Elder Thomas sits in the corner.

LIZ: You should have called an ambulance.
CHARLIE: With no health insurance?
LIZ: Being in debt is better than being dead. What's wrong with you? Why is there a Mormon here?
CHARLIE: Did I have a heart attack?
LIZ: No, you didn't have a heart attack.
    (Reading his blood pressure) Huh.
CHARLIE: What is it?

(Pause.)

LIZ: Tell me what you felt.
CHARLIE: Pain, in my chest. It was hard to breathe, I felt like I couldn't intake air.
LIZ: How are you sleeping?

CHARLIE: I'm tired all the time. I'm sleeping on the couch now actually, I can breathe better.

(Liz takes out a stethoscope. She checks his breathing.)

LIZ: You're wheezing.
CHARLIE: I always wheeze, Liz.
LIZ: You're wheezing more. Take a deep breath.

(Charlie takes a deep breath.)

Did that hurt?
CHARLIE: A little. What was my blood pressure?
LIZ: 238 over 134.

(Pause. Liz puts the stethoscope away.)

CHARLIE: Oh.
LIZ: Yeah. Oh.

(Pause.)

CHARLIE: Could you hand me my walker? I haven't been to the bathroom all day, I'm ready to explode.

(Liz hands him his walker, Charlie gets up with some effort. It's obvious he's having chest pain. Liz watches him.)

LIZ: You want help?
CHARLIE: No, I'm fine. Just—. Sorry.
LIZ: What are you sorry about?
CHARLIE: Sorry. I don't know. Sorry.

(Charlie makes his way to the bathroom, wheezing loudly. Elder Thomas and Liz look at one another.)

ELDER THOMAS: I should go.

LIZ: Thank you. For helping him. *(Pause)* You on your mission?

ELDER THOMAS: What?

LIZ: Is this your mission? You're on your mission now?

ELDER THOMAS: Oh—yeah.

LIZ: Where are you from?

ELDER THOMAS: Iowa.

LIZ: You grew up in Iowa and they sent you to *Idaho* on your mission?

ELDER THOMAS: Yeah, I don't know. Some of my friends got to go to Los Angeles. A few went to South America. It's—fine. *(Pause)* Is he going to be—?

LIZ: No. No, he's not.

ELDER THOMAS: He's sick?

LIZ: He's very, very, very sick. *(Pause)* I grew up Mormon.

ELDER THOMAS: Really? Oh, that's—that's actually nice to hear, I actually haven't run into a lot of others. Surprising, small town in Idaho, you'd think you'd . . . Do you go to the church over near the highway, or the—?

LIZ: I fucking hate Mormons. *(Small pause)* I shouldn't say that, I don't fucking hate Mormons, I fucking hate Mormon*ism*. How can you believe in a God like that? He gives us the Old Testament, fine, we'll all be Jews. Then Jesus shows up and he's like, "Hey so, I'm the son of God, stop being Jewish, here's the New Testament, sorry." And then he shows up a *second* time, and he's like, "Oh, shit, sorry! Here's this other thing, it's called the Book of Mormon." And after all that, we're still supposed to wait around for him to come back a *third fucking time* to kill us all with holy fire and dragons and—

ELDER THOMAS: That's a really unfair summary of my beliefs.

LIZ: I'm just saying, why would God not just give us all the right answers to begin with?

ELDER THOMAS: He has a plan.

LIZ: A plan that he's constantly revising.

ELDER THOMAS: I guess.

(Pause.)

LIZ: Look—it was good of you to stay with him. But if you're waiting around to convert him, or—

ELDER THOMAS: We don't "convert people." Our message is a message of hope for / people of all faiths—

LIZ: People of all faiths, I know, you're sweet. But he's not interested in what you have to say. It's the last thing he wants to hear. *(Lights up a cigarette)* Listen, you can go if you want. I know Charlie appreciates what you did.

ELDER THOMAS: He said he wanted to hear about the church.

(Pause.)

LIZ: Charlie said he wanted to hear about the church?

ELDER THOMAS: Yes.

(Pause.)

LIZ: No, he doesn't.

ELDER THOMAS: Why not?

LIZ: I just know.

ELDER THOMAS: How?

LIZ: Because it's caused him a lot of pain.

ELDER THOMAS: How?

LIZ: It killed his boyfriend.

(Pause.)

ELDER THOMAS: You're saying the church—

LIZ: —killed his boyfriend. Yes, the Church of Jesus Christ of Latter Day Saints killed Charlie's boyfriend. *(Pause)* And I should add that, personally, the Mormon Church has caused *me* a lot of pain in *my* life. That guy in there is the only person I have anymore that even resembles a friend, and I am not letting you come over here to talk to him. Especially not now, not this week.

ELDER THOMAS: Why not this week?

LIZ: Because he's probably not going to be here next week.

ELDER THOMAS: Where is he going?

(Charlie comes back out from the bathroom on his walker, moves toward the couch.)

CHARLIE: I'm sorry you had to come over, Liz. And I'm sorry—

LIZ: It's all right.

CHARLIE: I'm sorry that I always think I'm dying.

(Pause.)

LIZ: Charlie, your blood pressure is 238 over 134.

CHARLIE: That's not much more than it usually is.

LIZ: Yes, it is. And your normal blood pressure is at near-fatal levels as it is.

(Pause.)

CHARLIE: I'm sorry, I'm feeling better now. You can go back to—

LIZ: Go to the hospital.

CHARLIE: I'm sorry.

LIZ: Stop saying you're sorry. Go to the hospital.

CHARLIE: Liz—I'm sorry—

LIZ: I'm calling an ambulance and they're going to take you to the hospital!

CHARLIE: I can't!

LIZ: You're going to die, Charlie. You have congestive heart failure. If you don't go to the hospital, you will die. Probably before the weekend. You. Will. Die.

(Pause.)

CHARLIE: Then I should probably keep working, I have a lot of essays this week.

LIZ: GODAMMIT Charlie.

CHARLIE: I'm sorry. I'm sorry. I know, I'm—an awful person. I know. I'm sorry.

(Pause.)

ELDER THOMAS: Do you still want to hear about the church?

LIZ: NO. HE DOES NOT.

ELDER THOMAS: Okay. That's fine, I'm sorry, I—I'll go. *(Pause)* I still don't understand why you wanted me to read that essay to you.

(Pause.)

CHARLIE: It's a really good essay.

ELDER THOMAS: I actually thought it was pretty bad.

CHARLIE: It got a bad grade. But—it's a really, really good essay.

(Elder Thomas exits. A few beats pass.)

LIZ: Did you tell him you wanted to hear about the church?

CHARLIE: He's just a kid, Liz. He helped me out.

(Charlie grunts in pain, holding his chest a bit.)

LIZ: What?

CHARLIE: I'm fine.

LIZ: No, you're not.

(Pause.)

CHARLIE: I think—I need to call Ellie.

LIZ: Ellie?

CHARLIE: Yeah.

(Pause.)

LIZ: What, so you're like—giving up?

CHARLIE: What else am I supposed to do?

LIZ: Go to the hospital!

CHARLIE: Okay, I could go to the hospital. Get a bypass operation or whatever. Rack up several hundred thousand dollars of hospital bills that I won't be able to pay back, ever. Then I'll come back home, maybe, and last—what? A year? At the most? All so I could spend another year in what I'm sure is no small amount of pain.

LIZ: Nice positive thinking, Charlie. This affects me too, you know? You're my *friend*.

CHARLIE: I know. I'm sorry.

LIZ: You say you're sorry again, I'm going to shove a knife right into you, I swear to—

CHARLIE: Go ahead, what's it gonna do? My internal organs are two feet in at least.

(Pause. Liz laughs.)

LIZ: Fuck you.

(Charlie smiles. They look at one another.
Pause. Finally Liz sighs, goes to the couch and grabs the remote. She sits next to Charlie, puts her head on his shoulder.
She turns on the TV, flips through the channels absentmindedly.)

I've been telling you that this was gonna happen.

CHARLIE: Yeah.

LIZ: Haven't I been telling you—?

CHARLIE: Yes, I know. You have.

(*Pause.*)

LIZ: Well I'm not letting you just *die*. I don't care what you think, I'm not letting it happen.

(*Liz continues to flip through the channels. Silence.*)

CHARLIE: Did you bring anything?

(*Silence. Liz continues to flip channels.*)

Liz.

(*Liz flips a few more channels. Silence.*)

Please.

(*A few more channels. Silence. Then, without looking at Charlie, Liz goes to her bag and pulls out a large bucket of fried chicken. She goes to Charlie and puts it in his lap, keeping her eyes on the TV.*)

Thank you.

(*Charlie opens the bucket, eats. Liz continues to flip channels, then lands on one.*)

LIZ: *Judge Judy*, I've seen this one. It's good.

(*Charlie continues to eat, Liz watches the TV.*)

NIGHT

Charlie, alone, much later that night, eating the last piece of chicken from the bucket. The TV is on at a low level. As he finishes, he turns off the TV, staring forward silently for a moment.

CHARLIE *(Soft)*: "In the first part of his book, the author, calling himself Ishmael, is in a small seaside town and he is sharing a bed with a man named Queequeg."

(Charlie takes a breath, tries to make himself comfortable on the couch.)

"The author and Queequeg go to church and hear a sermon about Jonah, and later set out on a ship captained by the pirate named Ahab, who is missing a leg, and very much wants to kill the whale which is named Moby Dick, and which is white."

(Charlie breathes. He shifts on the couch, causing pain in is chest.)

"In the course of the book, the pirate Ahab encounters many hardships. His entire life is set around trying to kill a certain whale. I think this is sad because this whale doesn't have any emotions, and doesn't know how bad Ahab wants to kill him."

(Charlie settles into the couch, closes his eyes.)

"He's just a poor big animal. And I feel bad for Ahab as well, because he thinks that his life will be better if he can kill this whale, but in reality it won't help him at all. This book made me think about my own life. This book made me think about my own life. This book made me—"

(Lights quickly snap to black.
In the darkness, there is the faint sound of waves lapping against the shore—so quiet that it's nearly inaudible. The sound continues for a moment, rising just a bit in volume, becoming a bit more discernible, before lights rise on:)

Tuesday

Charlie sits on the couch. Ellie stands near the door. There is an awkward silence.

ELLIE: How much?

CHARLIE: I haven't been able to weigh myself in years, it's hard to know. Five-fifty? Six hundred?

ELLIE: That's disgusting.

CHARLIE: I know. It is disgusting, I'm sorry.

ELLIE: Does this mean I'm going to get fat?

CHARLIE: No, it doesn't. I was always big, but I just—let it get out of control.

(Pause.)

ELLIE: Who was the woman?

CHARLIE: What woman?

ELLIE: There was a woman in the background, when you called me.

CHARLIE: Oh, that's—my friend, Liz.

ELLIE: You have a friend?

CHARLIE: Yeah. She's a nurse, she used to do in-house calls for the hospice—

ELLIE: Is she, like, your fag hag? Because it seems like she could do a lot better.

(Pause.)

CHARLIE: Was your mom okay with you coming here?

ELLIE: I didn't tell her. She would've freaked out. *(Pause)* Why don't you just go to the hospital?

CHARLIE: I don't have health insurance.

ELLIE: But you might die.

CHARLIE: It's not worth it. *(Pause)* It's really good to see you. You look beautiful. How's school going? You're a senior, right?

ELLIE: You actually care?

CHARLIE: Of course I care. I pester your mom for information as often as she'll give it to me. *(Pause)* So why aren't—don't you have school?

ELLIE: Suspended until Friday.

CHARLIE: Oh. Why?

ELLIE: I blogged about my stupid bitch lab partner. She told her stupid bitch mom and the vice principal said it was "vaguely threatening."

CHARLIE: You don't like high school?

ELLIE: Only retards like high school.

CHARLIE: But—you're going to pass, right?

ELLIE: I'm failing most of my classes. My dumbass counselor says I might not graduate. I'm a smart person, I never forget anything. But high school is such bullshit. Busywork.

CHARLIE: It's important.

ELLIE: How would you know? *(Pause)* So, what? You want me to like help you clean yourself or go to the bathroom or something? Because if you need someone to help you do that stuff, then you need to find someone else.

CHARLIE: You don't need to do anything disgusting, I promise.

ELLIE: Just being around you is disgusting. You smell disgusting. Your apartment is disgusting. You look disgusting. The last time I saw you, you were disgusting.

CHARLIE: There's no way you could remember that. You were two years old.

ELLIE: I'm a smart person, I never forget anything. In the living room, with that old red couch and the TV with the wood frame. And you were on the floor, and Mom was screaming at you and you were just apologizing over and over, you were so pathetic. I remember that. Can I have one of those doughnuts?

(Small pause.)

CHARLIE: Yeah, sure.

(Ellie grabs a doughnut from a package sitting near the kitchen.)

ELLIE: You weren't all that heavy back then. I mean, you were fat, but not like this.

CHARLIE: Yeah.

ELLIE: Why did you gain all that weight?

(Pause.)

CHARLIE: I'd like us to spend some time together this week.

ELLIE: Why?

CHARLIE: We don't even know one another.

ELLIE: So?

(Pause.)

CHARLIE: I can pay you.

ELLIE: You want to pay me to spend time with you?

CHARLIE: And I can help you with your work. It's what I do for my job, I help people edit their essays—

ELLIE: Are you serious?

(Charlie picks up some essays sitting next to him.)

CHARLIE: It's what I do all day long. I can help you pass your classes.

ELLIE: How are you like, qualified to edit essays?

CHARLIE: I have a master's degree. In English, from the U of I. I teach online classes, it's my job.

ELLIE: You teach online?

CHARLIE: Yes.

ELLIE: Your students know what you look like?

(Pause.)

CHARLIE: I don't use a camera. Just a microphone.

ELLIE: That's probably a good idea. *(Pause)* Counselor dumbass says that if I show a lot of improvement in one subject that I might be able to pass. I can rewrite my old essays for credit, so you have to rewrite all of those, and write every other essay for the rest of the semester. And they have to be really good.

CHARLIE: I really shouldn't write them for you.

ELLIE: Well, it's what you're gonna do if you want me around. How much can you pay me?

CHARLIE: Whatever I have. All the money I have in the bank.

ELLIE: How much money do you have in the bank?

(Pause.)

CHARLIE: A hundred and twenty—

ELLIE: You want me to be here all week for a hundred and twenty dollars?

CHARLIE: Thousand. A hundred and twenty thousand dollars. *(Pause)* I never go out, I don't have health insurance, all I pay for is food, internet, three-fifty a month in rent. And I work all the time.

ELLIE: You'd give all that money to *me*? Not my mom, to *me*?

CHARLIE: Yes. All of it. Just—don't mention it to your mom. Okay? *(Pause)* Also . . . I'll write the essays for you, but I'd like you to do some writing yourself. Just for me. They don't have to be perfect, I'd just like you to write an essay or two for me.

ELLIE: Why?

CHARLIE: You're a smart person, I bet you're a strong writer. I want to know what you have to say. Plus, I'm a teacher. I want to make sure you're getting something out of this.

ELLIE: I don't even understand you.

(Silence.)

Stand up and walk over to me.

CHARLIE: What?

ELLIE: Come over here. Walk toward me. Come over here, beside me.

(Charlie pauses for a second, then reaches for his walker.)

Without that thing. Just stand up, and come over here.

CHARLIE: Ellie, I can't really—

ELLIE: Shut up. Come over here.

(Charlie takes a few deep breaths, then tries to stand on his feet.
He is unsuccessful at getting off the couch, and he begins to have severe chest pains. His breathing becomes quicker.
He tries again, this time he nearly gets up on his feet, but falls backward when the pain becomes unbearable. He is wincing from the pain, lying back on the couch, wheezing loudly.
Ellie stares at him, unmoved.)

NIGHT

Charlie sits on the couch. Liz is standing near Charlie, fiddling with a small machine with electrodes attached to it.

Liz has brought various bulk-sized groceries, they sit near the door still in bags.

LIZ: I don't remember what it's called, something ridiculous, I don't remember. But it's for you, it's going to help you out. This machine here, it senses perspiration. It's an indicator of stress. So the idea is, if you know what makes your stress level go up, you can learn to control it. And that'll reduce your heart rate, lower your blood pressure.

(Liz starts attaching the machine to Charlie's hand.)

CHARLIE: Where did you get this thing?
LIZ: Ginny, from the hospital, she's into this stuff.
CHARLIE: Do you know how to use it?

LIZ: If Ginny can figure it out, I'm sure it's not that hard. Here. *(Turns on the machine)* You see that number right there? That's how much you're sweating. You wanna try and make that number go down.

(Pause.)

CHARLIE: So what do I—?
LIZ: I don't know, just—relax. Take a deep breath. You're calm. You're very, very calm.

(Charlie takes a deep breath. Liz rubs his shoulders a bit, watching the machine.)

There, the number's going down. Isn't that better? It's about establishing a relationship between your brain and your body. Now you know you're calming yourself down because the little machine is telling you so.
CHARLIE: You really think this is going to help?
LIZ: Yes! It'll help, you just—need to do this all the time.

(Pause. Liz continues to rub his shoulders and watch the machine.)

CHARLIE: Ellie came over.

(Pause.)

LIZ: She did?
CHARLIE: Yes. *(Pause)* She's—amazing.
LIZ: Yeah?
CHARLIE: And—angry. Very angry. She's coming back tomorrow. I'm writing her essays for her, for school. She's failing most of her classes, I think. She's smart, I can tell she's smart, she just doesn't—
LIZ: Charlie, do you really—? You really think this is a good idea?

CHARLIE: What do you mean?

LIZ: Sorry, but you haven't seen this girl since she was two years old, and *now* you want to reconnect with her? By doing her homework for her?

CHARLIE: It's fine. It'll be fine.

LIZ: What is she gonna do if something happens to you, if you need help?

CHARLIE: I just want to spend some time with her, get to know her. I'm—worried about her.

LIZ: Why?

CHARLIE: She has this—website.

(Charlie takes the machine off his hand. He opens up his laptop and pulls up a website. Liz looks at the laptop.)

LIZ: I don't understand, what am I looking at?

CHARLIE: She calls it a "hate blog." She posts pictures of her friends, her mom even, and she just—insults them. The only thing she ever talks about is how much she doesn't like people.

LIZ: Huh. She's an angry little girl.

CHARLIE: Yes, she is. And I'm worried.

LIZ: She's just being a teenager. She'll be fine, she's got her mom to look out for her.

(Liz goes to her shopping bags, puts the food away in the kitchen as she talks.)

Listen, you shouldn't worry about her. When I was a kid—when my dad would really piss me off—I used to go to the supermarket over on Johnson, you remember that big place that used to be out there?

CHARLIE: Sure.

LIZ: I used to just—*trash* the place. And I was really good at it, I never got caught. I'd walk in really normally, wait until

I was in an aisle with no one in it, and then I'd—very quietly—destroy it. Open all the jars and boxes, spill everything on the floor. Pour out the milk, smash the produce under my feet. By the time I was done, they didn't know what hit them. Like this silent tornado had swept through the whole store. I was one angry little girl.

CHARLIE: You never told me about that.

LIZ: Yeah, well, it's not exactly a time in my life I love to think about, or—. *(Pause)* I'm just saying, you should be thankful that Ellie's doing this shit on the internet and not getting herself into real trouble.

(Liz takes an extra large meatball sub out of a shopping bag, brings it to Charlie. Charlie starts eating it, fairly quickly.)

Just don't get too worked up about this. You don't need anything stressing you out right now.

(Liz heads back to the kitchen.)

CHARLIE: I just want to make sure she's doing okay.

LIZ: She has a mother, Charlie. She's not alone, she has her mom.

CHARLIE: Well, she—

(Charlie stops, choking on the meatball sub. Liz remains in the kitchen, not noticing him.
Pause.
Charlie starts to panic.)

LIZ: What?

(No response.)

Charlie, you okay?

(Liz comes out of the kitchen, sees Charlie.)

Oh God. Oh God, are you choking?! You're choking?!

(Charlie leans forward as best he can, Liz hits his back a few times. It doesn't help.)

Okay, okay—lean over the arm!

(Charlie struggles to lean over the arm of the couch, stomach down. As best as she can, Liz pushes on Charlie's back, attempting the Heimlich maneuver. Finally, she puts all her weight into it, and Charlie spits out the piece of food.)

Shit. Oh, shit, Charlie.
CHARLIE *(Breathing heavily)*: I'm okay. I'm okay.

(Liz breathes. Charlie rolls back into a sitting position on the couch. Long pause.)

LIZ: GODDAMMIT CHARLIE, WHAT IS WRONG WITH YOU?
CHARLIE: I'm sorry—
LIZ: Chew your food like a normal human being! You could have choked to death just then, you realize that?! *You could have died right in front of me, you could have just—!*

(Silence. Liz breathes.)

CHARLIE: I'm sorry, Liz.

(Another silence. Liz calms down. She looks at her watch, then grabs the remote control, turning on the TV.)

LIZ: *House* is on. Preview looked good, a guy whose arm has a mind of its own, something like that. *(Pause)* You want a Dr. Pepper?

(Pause.)

CHARLIE *(Quietly)*: I'm sorry, Liz.
LIZ: I asked if you want a Dr. Pepper.

(Pause.)

CHARLIE *(Quieter)*: I'm sorry.

(Lights quickly snap to black.
   The sound of waves returns, this time just a bit louder, rising in volume until lights rise on:)

Wednesday

MORNING

Charlie sits in front of the laptop, as before, speaking into a microphone.

CHARLIE: A lot of you had some questions about my most recent assignment, so I just wanted to clear up some misconceptions. This is a new teaching strategy I'm trying out, so please bear with me. First, when I asked you to "make it more personal," I was not being "creepy" as Tina436 recently commented. And when I asked you to "not edit your bad grammar or potentially subjective, unspecific, or just plain stupid ideas," I had not gone "apeshit insane yo" as UNCMark45 recently commented. Do you all realize that I can access the class discussion forum? *(Pause)* Listen, at this point in this class, I've given you all I can in terms of structure, building a thesis, paragraph organization. But for once—just write it. See what happens. It won't count toward your final grade, you can rewrite it later if you want, I just—I want to know what you really think. Okay?

AFTERNOON

Charlie sits on the couch, Ellie sits in a chair on the other side of the room, typing on her iPhone. Charlie is reading an essay.

CHARLIE: This is . . . *(Pause)* You say here that Walt Whitman wrote *Song* for *Myself.*
ELLIE *(Not looking up)*: Yeah?
CHARLIE: It's called *Song* of *Myself.*
ELLIE: My title's better.

(Pause.)

CHARLIE: Yeah, well, it— . . . Okay, I'll just change it.

(Charlie writes something on the essay. He keeps reading.)

Okay. "In the poem *Song of Myself* by Walt Whitman, the author tells us how amazing he is. He tells us that he is better than everyone else, and that people should listen to what he says, because he is so wonderful."

ELLIE: You don't need to read it out loud. Just correct it.

CHARLIE: But it's not— . . . This really isn't what the poem is about.

ELLIE: Yes it is. I read it. It was really long and boring and it was about how great he thinks he is.

CHARLIE: But he's not really talking about himself, he's using the metaphor of "I" to refer to something a lot more universal. That's what's so amazing about the poem, on the surface it seems really self-involved and narcissistic, but actually it's about exploding the entire definition of the "self" in favor of this all-encompassing—

ELLIE: Oh my God I don't care.

(Pause.)

CHARLIE: You just want me to write it for you?

ELLIE: Yes.

CHARLIE: You don't want to understand the poem at all?

(Ellie finally looks up from her iPhone.)

ELLIE: You think I don't understand it?

CHARLIE: Well—

ELLIE: You're just like my idiot teachers. You think because I don't go nuts over some stupid little poem, it's because I'm too stupid to understand it.

CHARLIE: I didn't say that—

ELLIE: Maybe I *do* understand it. Maybe I understand *exactly* what this poem is about, but I just don't care. Because it was written by some self-involved moron, and even though he thinks that his "metaphor for the self" is deep and shit, it doesn't mean anything because he's just some worthless nineteenth-century faggot. How about that?

(Pause. They stare at one another.)

CHARLIE: That's an interesting perspective.

ELLIE: You think you're funny?

CHARLIE: It could make for an interesting essay.

ELLIE: Oh my God shut up. Just fix it, okay? Write that thing about "exploding the definition of self," my English teacher will love that.

(Ellie goes back to her iPhone. Charlie stares at her.)

CHARLIE: How's your mom doing?

ELLIE: Oh my God.

CHARLIE: I just thought we could—talk. A little.

ELLIE: If you're not going to write these essays for me, then I'm not gonna—

CHARLIE: Look, Ellie, I don't need you here to write this for you. I could write this essay in my sleep. And it's not fair of me to force you to stay here. If you really don't want to be here, you can go. You can still have the money.

(Pause. Ellie looks at Charlie.)

ELLIE: You'd let me have the money anyway?

CHARLIE: Yes.

ELLIE: I thought you wanted to get to know me.

CHARLIE: I do. But I don't want to force you to be here, that's not fair. It's up to you.

(Ellie looks at him for a moment, then puts away the iPhone.)

ELLIE: She's fine. Mom. I guess.

CHARLIE: Have you told her that you're coming over here?

ELLIE: No. She'd be pretty angry. Plus, she'd want the money.

CHARLIE: Is she—happy?

ELLIE: When she drinks.

CHARLIE: Oh. *(Pause)* Do you guys still live over in the duplex over on Orchard?

ELLIE: You don't even know where we live? How'd you get my cell phone number?

CHARLIE: Facebook.

ELLIE: Creepy. You don't stay in touch with Mom?

CHARLIE: Sometimes. She really only tells me things about you.

ELLIE: Why?

CHARLIE: Because that's all I ask about.

(Pause.)

ELLIE: When I was little we moved to an apartment on the other side of town, near the Circle K.

CHARLIE: Is your mother—with anyone now?

ELLIE: No. Why, you interested?

CHARLIE: Oh, no, I was just—

ELLIE: I'm kidding, Jesus. How could you be with anyone? *(Pause)* Why did you gain all that weight?

CHARLIE: Oh, that doesn't—

ELLIE: If you're gonna interrogate me, I get to do the same thing. Why did you gain all that weight?

(Pause.)

CHARLIE: Someone very close to me passed away, and it—had an effect on me.

ELLIE: Who was it?

CHARLIE: My . . .

(Charlie hesitates.)

ELLIE: Your boyfriend?

CHARLIE: Yes, my boyfriend. My partner.

ELLIE: What was his name?

CHARLIE: Alan.

ELLIE: How'd he die?

CHARLIE: He sort of . . . Slowly killed himself. *(Pause)* He had the flu, and it developed into pneumonia, but he got that sick because he—just sort of shut down. Stopped taking care of himself, stopped eating.

ELLIE: Why did he do that?

CHARLIE: He felt guilty. *(Quick pause)* I'd rather not talk about this right now, is that all right with you?

ELLIE: Whatever.

(Pause.)

CHARLIE: I'll fix this essay for you before you leave, but I'd like you to do a little writing for me. All right?

ELLIE: You were serious about that?

CHARLIE: Yes. Here.

(Charlie pulls out a notebook and a pen, hands them to Ellie.)

ELLIE: I hate writing essays.

CHARLIE: I know, just—be honest. Just think about the poem for a while, and write something. Write what you really think.

ELLIE: You want me to write what I really think?

CHARLIE: Yes. Don't worry about it being good, I'm the only person who will see it. *(Short pause)* Okay, I'm going to be in the bathroom for a while, but I'll start working on your essay after—

ELLIE: I'm not helping you to the bathroom.

CHARLIE: I didn't ask you to help.

(With a lot of effort, Charlie manages to stand up with his walker. He makes his way to the bathroom. Ellie starts writing absentmindedly. After a sentence or so, she gets bored. She opens up Charlie's laptop and starts looking around.)

A knock at the door.
Ellie is about to call for Charlie, then stops. She thinks for
a moment.
Ellie goes to the door, opening it. Elder Thomas stands in
the doorway.)

ELDER THOMAS: Oh, hi—uh. I'm . . . I was looking for Charlie?
ELLIE: He's in the bathroom.
ELDER THOMAS: Oh, okay. *(Short pause)* I can come back, if he—
ELLIE: No, it's fine. Come in.

(Elder Thomas comes inside, Ellie shuts the door behind him.)

ELDER THOMAS: Are you his—friend?
ELLIE: I'm his daughter.
ELDER THOMAS: Oh. Wow, I . . . I didn't know that.
ELLIE: You surprised?
ELDER THOMAS: Yes.
ELLIE: What's more surprising? That a gay guy has a daughter,
    or that someone found his penis?
ELDER THOMAS: I really should go.
ELLIE: Don't be a pussy. That nametag makes you look like a
    retard.
ELDER THOMAS: We—have to wear them.
ELLIE: I don't care. What are you doing here again? Who are
    you?
ELDER THOMAS: Charlie said he—wanted to hear about the
    church. I'm with the Church of Jesus Christ of Latter
    Day Saints. I came by the other day, he wasn't feeling
    well, I thought I'd try him again. I brought some reading
    materials, and I thought we could talk about—
ELLIE: I'm bored.
ELDER THOMAS: Oh.

(Pause.)

ELLIE: I'll tell you one thing I like about religion. What I like about religion is that it assumes everyone is an idiot and that they're incapable of saving themselves. I think they got something right with that.

ELDER THOMAS: That's not really what I—

ELLIE: I'm not finished talking. I'm saying that I appreciate how religion makes people realize that, I appreciate that. But what I don't like about religion is that once people accept Jesus or whatever, they think they're more enlightened than everyone else. Like, by accepting the fact that they're stupid sinners, they've become better than everyone else. And they turn into assholes.

(Pause.)

ELDER THOMAS: I don't really know what to say. I have some pamphlets—

ELLIE: Hold still.

ELDER THOMAS: What?

(Ellie takes out her iPhone, takes a picture of Elder Thomas.)

Why did you just do that?

ELLIE: Are you coming back tomorrow?

ELDER THOMAS: I don't—I'm not sure—

ELLIE: Come back tomorrow, I'll be here around the same time.

ELDER THOMAS: I'm sorry, what's happening?

(Charlie comes out of the bathroom with his walker, sees Elder Thomas.)

CHARLIE: Oh.

ELDER THOMAS: Hi, Charlie. I was just—

(Ellie takes a picture of Charlie, then puts the iPhone back in her bag.)

ELLIE: Will you have that done by tomorrow?
CHARLIE: Sure.
ELLIE: Five page minimum.
CHARLIE: I know. It'll be good, I promise.

(Ellie extends a hand to Elder Thomas.)

ELLIE: I'm Ellie.
ELDER THOMAS *(Shaking her hand)*: Elder Thomas.
ELLIE: Weird. See you later.

(Ellie exits. Charlie and Elder Thomas look at one another.)

ELDER THOMAS: Are you ready to hear about the church?

(Pause.)

CHARLIE: Yes.

Charlie sits in the same position as before, Elder Thomas holds some pamphlets. Charlie is glancing through one of them absentmindedly.

ELDER THOMAS: It was written by prophets, pretty much in the same way that the Bible was written. Through revelation and prophecy by the Nephite prophet Mormon, who lived in the Americas in the fourth century. He transcribed the history of his people onto a set of golden plates, and then hundreds of years later Joseph Smith, a man from upstate New York, translated the book from the gold plates in about sixty-five days or so—

CHARLIE: You go to the church near the highway, right? The older one, the one by the U-Haul?

ELDER THOMAS: Um—yeah. And to translate this book in sixty-five days is pretty remarkable because it means he had to translate the equivalent of about eight single-spaced pages per day—

CHARLIE: What's your name?

(Pause.)

ELDER THOMAS: I told you. It's Elder Thomas.
CHARLIE: But what's your real name?
ELDER THOMAS: Thomas.
CHARLIE: That's your last name, right? What's your first name?
ELDER THOMAS: You don't need to know my first name.
CHARLIE: Oh.

(Pause.)

ELDER THOMAS: What's also really incredible is that the Book of Mormon actually contains many distinct literary styles, including ancient Hebrew poetry and—
CHARLIE: Why is that incredible?
ELDER THOMAS: Well, it—how would some farmboy living in upstate New York have known how to write in the style of ancient Hebrew poetry? It's living proof of God's intervention.
CHARLIE: Hm. *(Pause)* You know, actually—I know all this.
ELDER THOMAS: What do you mean?
CHARLIE: I've read just about every Wikipedia article about Mormonism—
ELDER THOMAS: I don't know if Wikipedia is the best source for—
CHARLIE: I also read the Book of Mormon.
ELDER THOMAS: The whole thing?
CHARLIE: Sure. A couple times.

(Pause.)

ELDER THOMAS: Did you—like it?
CHARLIE: I thought it was . . . Devastating.
ELDER THOMAS: Huh. Okay. I don't know about that.

CHARLIE: That one story about—Sherem? Sherem was questioning whether Jesus was actually God, so God struck Sherem
down. And Sherem repented as he was dying, said that he
was wrong, and so everyone believed in Jesus. God killed
this man to—prove a point. That story, it's—devastating.

ELDER THOMAS: Yeah, that—I never thought about it like that,
but— *(Pause)* You know what I think is amazing? The
Bible is great and everything, I mean—it's a really great
way to come to understand God. But it's so—distant. This
thing written thousands of years ago, on the other side of
the planet, in languages we don't speak. It's been translated and translated, probably rewritten over and over and
over. But the Book of Mormon—it's like, a *direct link* to
God's word. One translator, writing in English, right here
in America, just a few generations ago. It's—

CHARLIE: Devastating.

ELDER THOMAS: No. No, it's—hopeful. It makes you feel like
there's some meaning to being here, right now, in America. Do you see that? *(Pause)* You're so close in time and
space to God's revelation, Charlie, that should make you
feel proud. It should inspire you. It should keep you from
doing this to yourself.

(Pause.)

CHARLIE: I'm not interested in converting, Elder Thomas.
I don't find the Mormon Church hopeful. I don't find it
amazing, and I don't find the proof convincing.

ELDER THOMAS: Wait so why did you want me to—? *(Pause)*
Um. I want to just make sure that—. I want to make sure
you know that I'm just coming over here to talk about the
church. That's it.

CHARLIE: Well, yeah. What?

ELDER THOMAS: I just . . . I don't know if—
(Pause, then suddenly) You're not attracted to me, right?

charlie: Oh my God.

elder thomas: It's just, with the—. What you were watching, the first time I came in here—

charlie: I am not attracted to you. Please, understand me when I say that. *I am not attracted to you. You're a fetus.* *(Pause)* Is that what you really think of me?

elder thomas: *No,* I—

charlie: No, really. Tell me the truth. Do you find me disgusting?

(Pause.)

elder thomas: No. *(Pause)* It's just that—you said you wanted to hear about the church.

charlie: I did want to hear about the church. Your church, the one by the U-Haul, near the highway. I wanted to hear about *that* church.

elder thomas: I don't understand.

charlie: You can go now, I'm sorry if I—

elder thomas: Is this about your—? Your domestic— . . .

charlie: How do you know about—?

elder thomas: Your friend, Liz—she told me, she said that your—whatever, he had gone to the church?

charlie: Look, you don't want to hear about this, you're just a kid—

elder thomas: I'm not a kid, I'm nineteen. *(Pause)* Charlie— I've been going door to door for a while, you know? But no one understands that—I want to get to know them. The good and the bad, everything. How are we supposed to talk about your spiritual life if I don't know anything about who you are?

(Pause. Charlie considers for a moment.)

charlie: His name—my partner's name, it was Alan. *(Pause)* It sounds strange, but he was actually a student of mine.

He was only a couple years younger than me, he had gone back to school after his mission. His parents were trying to get him to marry someone from the church, I think he barely knew her. But he was gonna go through with it—until he met me. It was ridiculous, he was the engaged son of a Mormon bishop, I had a wife and kid at home. But we just—couldn't stand to be apart. *(Pause)* You really want me to keep going?

ELDER THOMAS: Yes. Really, yes.

CHARLIE: I thought he'd be able to get over all this religious stuff, but— . . . It got worse and worse, to the point where every time we'd drive by that church near the highway he'd start to hyperventilate. His parents had abandoned him, refused to talk to him at all. But one night, about ten years ago, his father showed up here and told Alan he just wanted him to go to church the next day. He said, "I'm giving the talk tomorrow and I've written it for you. If you never come again—just come to church tomorrow." I told Alan not to go, but . . . The next morning he came home afterward, and he was just—hollow. It took him over, and he just—stopped everything. He stopped bathing, he stopped eating, he stopped sleeping. And a few months later, he was gone.

ELDER THOMAS: What happened? At the service?

CHARLIE: I don't know. Alan wouldn't tell me what they did to him. I guess—I was hoping you could find out.

(Pause.)

ELDER THOMAS: I don't—I'm not even from here, I don't know if—

CHARLIE: I know—never mind. It's ridiculous.

(Pause.)

ELDER THOMAS: I'm going to ask around, all right? I'll see if anyone remembers that day, the last day he was there. Who knows, someone might remember.

CHARLIE: You'd do that?

ELDER THOMAS: Of course. I just want to help. That's why I'm on a mission in the first place, right?

(Liz enters through the door with an extra wide wheelchair and a shopping bag.)

LIZ: All right, I got you something. I did some asking around, and this doctor said—

(Liz notices Elder Thomas.)

What the hell, Charlie?

ELDER THOMAS: I was just—

LIZ: *Charlie?*

CHARLIE: It's fine, Liz.

LIZ: What did I say about your stress level? You don't need someone coming over and telling you that you're going to hell.

ELDER THOMAS: I never said that, I would never say that.

LIZ: Leave.

CHARLIE: Liz—

LIZ: *Get out.*

ELDER THOMAS: Okay.

(Elder Thomas heads for the door.)

CHARLIE: Liz, stop it. He didn't do anything to you, for Christ's sake. He's just a kid.

ELDER THOMAS: I'm nineteen. *(Pause)* I'll just go—

LIZ: Actually—stay. We'll have a chat. *(To Charlie)* I brought you this.

CHARLIE: Thank you. What is it?

LIZ: What the fuck does it look like? It's a fat guy wheelchair.

CHARLIE: Why do I need a wheelchair?

LIZ: I was talking to one of the ER doctors, he told me that moderate activity would be a good idea. That a sense of independence would help you keep your spirits up. Now you don't have to sit on that couch all day long.

CHARLIE: How much did you pay for this thing?

LIZ: Nothing. We ordered it 'specially for a patient a few months ago, it's just been sitting around.

CHARLIE: What happened to the patient?

LIZ: Try it out. Now you can go to the bedroom by yourself, get to the bathroom more easily.

(Liz moves the wheelchair next to Charlie.
Charlie braces himself on his walker and manages to pull himself up.
Liz positions the wheelchair behind Charlie, Charlie starts slowly backing into the wheelchair.)

(Like a truck backing up) Beep. Beep. Beep. Beep.

(Charlie stops, looks back at her. Liz smiles.
Charlie continues, then sits in the wheelchair, wheezing loudly. He tries it out, wheeling himself a few feet.)

Good?

CHARLIE: Yeah, it's—. It's actually nice.

(Rolls a few more feet.)

Thank you, Liz, it's really—

LIZ: Why don't you see if it fits through the bedroom door, you probably haven't been in there for days, right?

ELDER THOMAS: I should probably go—

LIZ: Not before we have our little chat.

ELDER THOMAS: Oh, I. What?

CHARLIE: Liz—

LIZ *(To Charlie)*: Give us a few minutes.

(Liz pushes him toward the bedroom, out of the room. Liz turns back to Elder Thomas, stares at him.)

Take a seat.

(Elder Thomas sits down.)

So. Iowa?

ELDER THOMAS: What?

LIZ: You're from Iowa.

ELDER THOMAS: Uh. Yes.

LIZ: What part?

ELDER THOMAS: Waterloo?

LIZ: You asking me?

ELDER THOMAS: No, I—I'm from Waterloo.

(Pause. Liz smokes.)

LIZ: So listen. You're just a kid, you don't know anything. But I want to be very clear with you about a few things if you're going to keep coming over here. *(Pause)* I know this is fun for you. You get to travel around, act superior to everyone else. Plus you get to go home, get married, get some boring job, have tons of kids, and when you die you get your own planet. It all sounds pretty awesome. But, there are other kinds of people. People like Charlie, for whom this amazing plan doesn't fit. You can't fit a round peg in a square hole, and you certainly can't fit a morbidly obese gay peg in a Mormon hole. That came out wrong. *(Pause)* Point is—you're a sweet kid, but he doesn't need this right now.

ELDER THOMAS: I disagree.

(Pause.)

LIZ: Excuse me?

ELDER THOMAS: Sorry, I just—I think this is exactly what he needs right now. He's refusing to go to the hospital, he's dying—what he needs is some spiritual guidance.

LIZ: And you're gonna give him that?

ELDER THOMAS: No. God will.

LIZ: I see. *(Pause)* My big brother went on a mission. Went to Switzerland.

ELDER THOMAS: Oh.

LIZ: Yeah. He was the good kid. I however was the black sheep—by the time I was thirteen, I refused to go to church, told my dad I didn't believe in God. Even had to move out of the house, went to live with my aunt and uncle in Boise until I graduated. But not my big brother— he was a good Mormon.

He wrote me a letter a few months into his mission, he told me he was cold all the time. That he was cold all the time, and lonely, but he preferred being out there in Switzerland because he didn't want to come back and get married.

ELDER THOMAS: He didn't want to—?

LIZ: Dad had set it all up, pushed him into getting engaged to this girl from the church he barely knew. When he came back, he refused to go through with the wedding. Fell in love with someone else, started a whole new life. Until one day, when he went back to the church—I don't know what the hell they did to him that day, but it sure fucked him up. And after that he just started wasting away until he was just—gone. *(Pause)* That was my brother. Alan. My big brother who was *crushed* under the church that you think can save Charlie.

53

ELDER THOMAS: Oh.

(Silence. Liz stares at him, smoking.)

I'm sorry.

LIZ: What the fuck are you sorry about? *(Pause)* Where's your companion?

ELDER THOMAS: What?

LIZ: You always have to be in pairs. I know that. It's sort of a big deal for you to be out here alone, isn't it?

(Pause.)

ELDER THOMAS: Elder Johnson. He's—not feeling well.

LIZ: Not feeling well?

ELDER THOMAS: Why does it matter?

LIZ: It's a pretty big deal for you guys not to—

ELDER THOMAS: Well, to be honest, he's having some—problems and he's pretty useless right now, but I thought I could do some good. By myself. Help just *one* person.

LIZ: And that one person is Charlie.

ELDER THOMAS: Yes.

(Charlie comes out of the bedroom. Liz doesn't notice him.)

LIZ: Listen to me. He doesn't need your help, he doesn't want saving. In a few days he's probably going to be dead, and right now what he needs is for you to leave him alone. I am the only person who knows how to take care of him, do you understand? *I am the only one who can save him.*

CHARLIE: Liz.

(Liz turns around, sees Charlie. Elder Thomas quickly gathers his things and exits. Liz forces a smile.)

LIZ: Everything go all right in there?

(No response.)

I've got an hour or so before I need to get back, we could watch some *Maury*. Wheel yourself over here, c'mon.

(Liz turns on the TV. Charlie stares at her, not moving.)

NIGHT

Charlie, alone, in his wheelchair. He is laying some blankets out for the night onto the couch. He's about to move onto the couch when he notices Ellie's notebook. He wheels himself over to it, picks it up, opens it.

CHARLIE *(Reading)*: "This apartment smells. This notebook is retarded. I hate everyone."

(Charlie looks at it for a moment, smiling.)

"This apartment smells. This notebook is retarded. I hate everyone."

(Charlie laughs a little. The laugh quickly turns into a cough, which produces pain in his chest. He takes a few breaths, trying to calm himself down.)

(Soft) "I felt saddest of all when I read the boring chapters that were only descriptions of whales, because I knew that

the author was just trying to save us from his own sad story, just for a little while. This apartment smells."

(Charlie takes a few deep breaths, wheezing. The pain starts to subside.)

"This apartment smells. This notebook is retarded. I hate everyone. The author was just trying to save us from his own sad story, just for a little while. I hate everyone. The author was just trying to—"

(Lights quickly snap to black.

In the darkness, once again we hear the sound of waves—louder now, and more distinct, building a little in volume before lights rise on:)

Thursday

Charlie sits in the wheelchair, in front of his laptop, speaking into the microphone.

CHARLIE: KimmyBallz429, I read your recent post on the discussion forum about strategies for coming up with a good thesis. You said that I want you to "just pick a sentence from the book and say it's good or some shit." *(Pause)* I think I owe you all an apology. I've been teaching you all to rewrite and rewrite and rewrite, to edit your thoughts and change them and make them clearer, more precise, more objective. And I'm starting to realize that that's horseshit. You don't have any true reaction to these books because I've taught you to edit your reactions, to reshape them and reconfigure them over and over. And after all that, you don't even have a reaction at all. You just end up hating it. *(Pause)* How about this? Don't write about the book. Forget the assignment, forget the readings. Hell, forget everything you know about what makes a good essay and just—write. Just sit down, and write me something. Just give me something honest. Okay?

Ellie stands by the door, holding an essay.

ELLIE: So it's good?
CHARLIE: It's really, really good.
ELLIE: What grade am I gonna get?
CHARLIE: It's a really good essay.
ELLIE: Yeah, whatever. Okay bye.

   (Ellie turns to the door.)

CHARLIE: I was hoping you could write a little more in your
   notebook.
ELLIE: Oh my God.
CHARLIE: You've only written a couple sentences so far—could
   you write me some more?
ELLIE: I kind of hate you.
CHARLIE: Yeah, but you hate everyone. *(Pause)* Look, just keep
   going with what you were doing. Forget the poem, forget

about writing an essay. Just keep going, write about whatever you want, whatever you're thinking—

ELLIE: Shut up, just give me the notebook.

(Charlie hands Ellie the notebook. She sits down, opening it. She is about to write, then looks at Charlie.)

My mom found out. That I'm coming here.

(Pause.)

CHARLIE: How?

ELLIE: Small town bullshit. Her friend Judy saw the car parked outside here. *(Pause)* She asked me how big you were.

CHARLIE: She knows that I—?

ELLIE: She just heard you gained weight. She doesn't know you're a monster. *(Pause)* She made me promise to stop coming over.

CHARLIE: Did you tell her about the money?

ELLIE: I'm not retarded.

(Pause. Ellie writes a bit, Charlie watches her.)

CHARLIE: I was in a strange place in my life when I married your mom.

ELLIE: Did I fucking ask?

CHARLIE: Sorry. I just thought you . . . I'm sure your mom has told you the whole story anyway.

ELLIE: No, she hasn't, she doesn't like talking about you. Ever. But I'm pretty sure I know the story anyway. You come home one day, "Oh, honey, I'm so repressed, I need to self-actualize" or some stupid shit. And Mom starts screaming, then you're on the floor, just like I remember, looking pathetic and fat. Is that it?

(Pause.)

CHARLIE: I understand that you're angry.

ELLIE: Oh my God.

CHARLIE: But you don't need to be angry at the entire world. I'm the asshole, just be angry at me, don't take it out on—

ELLIE: You think you're the only person who's ever fucked me over? Trust me, I have a list. And you're no more important than any other asshole that's treated me like dirt.

(Ellie goes back to writing. Charlie watches her. A few moments pass.)

You could have sent her money, you know.

CHARLIE: What?

ELLIE: If you have all that money. You could have been sending money to my mom.

CHARLIE: I did.

ELLIE: I mean more than just child support.

(Long silence.)

CHARLIE: I did. *(Pause)* I'm so sorry, Ellie. I'm so, so sorry.

(Ellie looks up at Charlie for a second, then goes back to writing. A few moments pass. Ellie puts the pen down, looks at Charlie.)

ELLIE: I'm hungry.

(Pause.)

CHARLIE: There's stuff for sandwiches in the kitchen.

ELLIE: Okay. *(Pause)* I'll make you one, but it's going to be small. And I'm only using turkey or chicken, and no mayonnaise.

(Pause.)

CHARLIE: Thank you.

(Ellie gets up, goes toward the kitchen.)

What were you writing about?
ELLIE: I was writing about how when you die, you won't fit through the door or the windows. So they'll probably have to take you out in pieces.

(Ellie exits into the kitchen.)

AFTERNOON

Charlie is asleep in his wheelchair. Ellie is sitting on the couch typing on Charlie's laptop, smoking pot from a small glass pipe.
   A knock at the door.
   Ellie puts the pipe in Charlie's hand. Charlie doesn't wake up.

ELLIE: Yeah?
ELDER THOMAS *(From outside)*: I, uh—hello?

   (Ellie pauses for a second, recognizing the voice, then takes the pipe out of Charlie's hand. She goes to the door, opening it. Elder Thomas stands in the doorway holding his bicycle helmet.)

ELLIE: What?
ELDER THOMAS: Oh, I—
ELLIE: What?
ELDER THOMAS: Hi. *(Sees the pipe)* Are you—?
ELLIE: I'm bored. Come inside.
ELDER THOMAS: Maybe I should—

ELLIE: Oh my God stop talking. Take that nametag off, I told you, you look like a retard.

(Ellie closes the door behind Elder Thomas.)

ELDER THOMAS *(Seeing Charlie)*: Is he . . . ?

ELLIE: Do you ever finish sentences? He's asleep.

ELDER THOMAS: I can come back.

ELLIE: He'll be asleep for a while.

ELDER THOMAS: Oh. Is he okay?

ELLIE: I don't know. I ground up some Ambien and put it in his sandwich.

ELDER THOMAS: Oh my God, is he—?

ELLIE: I only gave him a couple, he's fine. I can take three at a time.

ELDER THOMAS: Why did you—? You have Ambien? Where did you get Ambien?

ELLIE: I had sex with a pharmacist. Just kidding, gross. My mom eats them like Tic Tacs. Do you ever wear anything different?

ELDER THOMAS: Should he be taking sleeping pills? He's sort of sick and—

ELLIE: Yeah, anyway. Why is your name "Elder"?

ELDER THOMAS: It's not my real . . . During the mission, we all get called "Elder." My last name is Thomas, so—I'm Elder Thomas.

ELLIE: It makes you sound, like, important. Which you're not.

(Ellie sits down, takes a hit from the pipe. Elder Thomas watches.)

ELDER THOMAS: No, I'm not.

ELLIE: Does this make you nervous?

ELDER THOMAS: No, I—. Well, yeah, it does.

ELLIE: It's just pot, it's not like I'm smoking crack or anything. You probably have no idea what I'm talking about.

ELDER THOMAS: Don't—. I know what you're talking about. I know what drugs are.

ELLIE: You only think you know what drugs are because your parents told you a whole bunch of lies about them. You probably think that smoking pot will turn you into a homeless person or something.

ELDER THOMAS: You know, I'm not an idiot. I've smoked pot before.

ELLIE: Oo, I'm so impressed.

ELDER THOMAS: I'm not trying to impress you, I'm just saying—

ELLIE: You have not smoked pot.

ELDER THOMAS: Yes, I have. It was—kind of a problem.

ELLIE: A "problem"?

ELDER THOMAS: My bishop told me I had an addiction.

ELLIE: That is the stupidest fucking thing I have ever heard in my entire life.

(Ellie takes a hit, holds it in.)

ELDER THOMAS: I was doing it every day. I had a problem.

ELLIE: You were a stoner. You had a hobby.

(Ellie exhales, blowing the hit in Elder Thomas's face.)

ELDER THOMAS: Okay, I'm leaving.

ELLIE: If you leave, I'll feed him the rest of the pills I have in the bottle.

(Elder Thomas stops.)

ELDER THOMAS: What?

ELLIE: There's probably twenty or thirty more. I'll crush them up and mix them into some water and pour it down his throat.

ELDER THOMAS: Why would you say something like that?

ELLIE: Sit down.

ELDER THOMAS: You wouldn't really do that, would you?

ELLIE: Oh my God sit down.

(Elder Thomas pauses, then sits down on the couch.)

Why do you keep coming back here?

ELDER THOMAS: He wants me to come over, he told me. He needs help.

ELLIE: That's a stupid reason. Take a hit.

ELDER THOMAS: What? No.

ELLIE: You've never smoked before.

ELDER THOMAS: Yes, I have.

ELLIE: You're some sheltered little Mormon boy, you haven't done anything. You don't know anything. God, I can't even look at you.

ELDER THOMAS: Why do you talk like that, is this how you treat everyone?

ELLIE: Yeah. Why does he want to talk to you?

ELDER THOMAS: I think he needs God to be in his life right now.

ELLIE: That's an even stupider reason. Do you think he wants to have sex with you? That's so gross, oh my God. Take a hit.

ELDER THOMAS: He doesn't want to—! I don't want to take a hit!

ELLIE: Why are you such a *pussy?* You wear a *bicycle helmet.* Take a hit.

(Ellie shoves the pipe into Elder Thomas's chest.)

ELDER THOMAS: I told you—

ELLIE: If you don't take a hit, I'm going to call the police and tell them you tried to rape me. Take a hit.

(Pause.)

67

ELDER THOMAS: I don't understand you at all.
ELLIE: Oh my God.

(Elder Thomas takes the pipe.)

ELDER THOMAS: Is there a carb on this?
ELLIE: Oo, I'm so impressed.
ELDER THOMAS: I wasn't trying to—
ELLIE: There isn't a carb.

(Elder Thomas takes a hit. He exhales. Ellie takes out her iPhone and snaps a quick picture Elder Thomas as he exhales.)

ELDER THOMAS *(Coughing)*: What are you doing? Why did you just—?
ELLIE: Calm down. Take another hit.
ELDER THOMAS: What are you going to do with that picture?
ELLIE: I'm gonna masturbate to it, is that what you want me to say? You're a pervert. Take another hit.

(No response. Elder Thomas stares at her.)

Look, I'm just fucking with you, all right? I'm not gonna kill anyone, I'm not gonna tell anyone you raped me. I don't understand why people believe everything I say. People are such idiots, it's so easy, it's ridiculous.
ELDER THOMAS: You aren't going to feed him more Ambien?
ELLIE: No.
ELDER THOMAS: Did you really put some in his sandwich?
ELLIE: That I did. Just a couple. So he'd stop bugging me.
ELDER THOMAS: Why don't you just leave?
ELLIE: I don't know.
ELDER THOMAS: If you hate him so much why do you keep coming over?
ELLIE: I'm done answering questions now.

ELDER THOMAS: Okay.

(Silence.)

Can I have another hit?

ELLIE: It goes against your religion, and that makes you a hypocrite. Go ahead.

(Elder Thomas takes another hit—a big one.)

ELDER THOMAS: I never really thought I had a problem. I did it every day for a while, then I stopped. If I was able to stop then how is it a problem?

ELLIE: That's the only smart thing you've said since you came in here.

ELDER THOMAS: This is really good weed.

ELLIE: No it's not. You just haven't smoked in a while.

(Ellie takes another picture of him.)

ELDER THOMAS: I really wish you wouldn't do that.

ELLIE: Yeah, I heard you the first time. Do you find me attractive?

ELDER THOMAS: I—

ELLIE: Because I'm not attracted to you at all, just to let you know.

(Pause.)

ELDER THOMAS: Okay.

ELLIE: I'm not trying to be mean or anything. But I just don't think you're good looking or interesting. Or intelligent.

ELDER THOMAS *(A little hurt)*: Oh.

ELLIE: Oh my God grow up. Maybe someone else finds you attractive, just not me. Maybe my dad finds you attractive.

ELDER THOMAS: I really wish you wouldn't say that.

69

ELLIE: It's so easy to make you uncomfortable, it's a little sad.
    You can cash that out.
ELDER THOMAS: You don't mind?
ELLIE: No.

*(Elder Thomas takes another big hit from the pipe. He's pretty
high by this point.)*

ELDER THOMAS: I don't know if I'm going to be able to bike
    back to my apartment.
ELLIE: Wow, you're pretty high, aren't you?
ELDER THOMAS: Yes. Yes, I am. And if my parents knew I was
    getting high, that I was getting high while I was on my
    mission—
ELLIE: You're not on a mission.

(Pause.)

ELDER THOMAS: What?
ELLIE: I said you're not on a mission. Jesus. *(Pause)* I remem-
    bered your name from your nametag. The Mormon web-
    site has a search engine for, like, everything. Anyway,
    there was a list of twelve people on missions in northern
    Idaho, and you're not one of them.

(Pause.)

ELDER THOMAS: They didn't update the website.
ELLIE: I'm not a retard.

(Pause.)

ELDER THOMAS: I need to go.
ELLIE: You keep saying that. Why are you pretending to be a
    Mormon missionary?

ELDER THOMAS: I'm not—I *am* on a mission—
ELLIE: Oh my God.
ELDER THOMAS: I mean I—*was*. I was on a mission.
ELLIE: Here?
ELDER THOMAS: I have to go.

(Elder Thomas stands up, a little shaky on his feet.)

ELLIE: What happened?
ELDER THOMAS: *Why do you care?!*
ELLIE: Because I think we have a blossoming friendship.

(Pause. Elder Thomas looks at her.)

ELDER THOMAS: I thought you said I wasn't attractive or interesting or intelligent.
ELLIE: So?
ELDER THOMAS: So why would you want to be my friend?
ELLIE: Because everyone else I know is even less attractive, interesting and intelligent than you.

(Pause.)

ELDER THOMAS: You won't tell anyone?
ELLIE: Who am I gonna tell?

(Pause. Elder Thomas sits back down on the couch next to Ellie.)

ELDER THOMAS: I was in eastern Oregon, in Pendleton. It's where they do that big annual rodeo, the famous one—
ELLIE: I really, really don't care about that.
ELDER THOMAS: Anyway, I was on my mission there. Last year.
ELLIE: What happened?
ELDER THOMAS: I left. I didn't want to do it anymore. *(Pause)* We just kept trying to talk to people, really *engage* with

them, but most of the time they'd just talk to us for a little while, say "thank you," and we'd never hear from them again. So after a while, it was like—what am I *actually doing* here? Am I really, like, really *helping* people?

ELLIE: No you were not.

ELDER THOMAS: I started to feel that way, too.

ELLIE: I don't *feel* that way, I *know* that you weren't helping people. Like, for a fact. It doesn't help people to tell them how to believe in God. Why would that help people?

ELDER THOMAS: It might bring them eternal salvation. *(Pause)* Maybe.

ELLIE: "Maybe"? You're shitty at being a religious person.

ELDER THOMAS: I just—I *want* to believe it. My family, all my friends, they seem like—totally happy. I wanna be like that.

ELLIE: So why did you come to Idaho?

ELDER THOMAS: I got kicked off the mission.

ELLIE: For smoking pot?

ELDER THOMAS: For assaulting my companion.

(Pause.)

ELLIE: You're full of shit.

ELDER THOMAS: No, I'm not.

ELLIE: Oh my God you so are.

ELDER THOMAS: Seriously.

ELLIE: So what, like, you went on a "pot bender"?

ELDER THOMAS: I wasn't smoking at all. The moment I stepped foot in Oregon, I made a promise to myself that I wouldn't smoke anymore. And I didn't.

ELLIE: Which is a shame if it's your first time in Oregon. So why did you beat him up?

ELDER THOMAS: He just . . . He didn't care. About anything. We'd go out every day, we'd try to talk to people, and no one would listen, and he *didn't even care*. I tried to talk to him about different sections of town we could go to, different ways to engage them, different ways to *help* these people . . . But you could tell, if we spent our whole mission there ministering and hadn't helped *one single person*, he wouldn't have cared. His faith was just—. He didn't need to earn it or prove it *at all*. And one day, we were out in this little farming community, and we weren't helping anyone, and he kept complaining about being hungry, and how hot it was out that day, and—I just lost it. I went nuts. *(Pause)* He told me his parents would sue me, that I'd go to jail. All I wanted to do was finish this mission, I wanted to see Mormonism help *one person*. So, I just got on a bus. I still have a few thousand dollars left in my checking account. I went to the church here in town a couple times, I found this nametag in the common room.

(Pause. Ellie looks at him.)

ELLIE: So what's your real name?
ELDER THOMAS: Why do you want to know?
ELLIE: Because we're friends now.

(Pause.)

ELDER THOMAS: Joseph Paulson.

(Ellie takes a picture of him.)

ELLIE: You're slightly more interesting now.
ELDER THOMAS: Thank you.

(The door bursts open revealing Mary, a woman of about forty but who looks considerably older.)

ELLIE: Shit.

(Mary pushes in, past Ellie and Elder Thomas, sees Charlie. She stops immediately. Long silence as she stares at Charlie. She moves toward him slowly.)

Mom—
MARY: Shut up.

(She stands next to Charlie, looking down at him.)

Charlie.

(Charlie doesn't move.)

Charlie.

(No response. Mary looks at Ellie. Ellie looks away.)

ELLIE: Yeah okay sorry.

LATE AFTERNOON

Charlie sits in his wheelchair, awake but very groggy. Liz is attaching an oxygen tank to the wheelchair and running a hose over his ears and under his nose. Mary sits on the couch smoking a cigarette. Ellie stands by the door, Elder Thomas in the opposite corner.

Throughout the scene, Charlie's breathing is much more shallow, and his wheezing is much worse.

LIZ *(To Mary)*: You know, he's not breathing so good. Second-hand smoke isn't really a great idea.
CHARLIE: She's fine, Liz.
LIZ: What, are you a doctor?
MARY: No, and neither are you.

(Mary puts out the cigarette in an empty soda can. She stares at Charlie.)

LIZ: Are you having more pain?
CHARLIE: Yes. Wheezing's getting worse.

LIZ: How easy is it to move?

CHARLIE: Not very.

LIZ: How about any confusion? Have you felt disoriented, confused, forgotten where you are or what you're doing?

CHARLIE: No. Would that be bad?

LIZ: Yes. That would be very bad.

CHARLIE: So—am I okay?

LIZ: No, you're not "okay." But as far as the sleeping pills, you're fine. I think she only gave you a couple.

ELLIE: Yeah, that's what I told you.

(Liz takes off the stethoscope, moves toward Ellie.)

LIZ: Listen to me. I was a very angry, very stupid little girl once too, but this goes beyond smoking pot and posting shit on the internet. If you would have given him more pills than that, you could have—

ELLIE: Yeah, except I didn't give him more than that, I gave him *two pills.*

MARY *(To Ellie)*: Ellie, how much money did he offer you?

CHARLIE: Mary. Don't.

MARY *(To Charlie)*: All of it? It would have to be all of it. It would take quite a lot of money to make that girl do something she doesn't want to do.

ELLIE: How do you know about—?

MARY *(To Ellie)*: You think I'm an idiot? You think for one second I would believe that you were coming here out of the kindness of your heart?

ELLIE: You're not getting any of it. He said I could have all of it.

LIZ: Charlie doesn't have any money.

(Pause.)

MARY: What?

LIZ: I do all his shopping, I know exactly how much is in his checking account.

(Pause.)

MARY *(To Charlie)*: She doesn't know?

CHARLIE: Mary—

MARY *(To Liz)*: Where do you think all the money from his teaching has been going? The account for Ellie—by now it has to be huge. *(To Charlie)* Over a hundred thousand at least, right?

LIZ *(To Charlie)*: That isn't true, is it? *(Pause)* Charlie, we could have gotten you anything you needed—special beds, physical therapists, fucking *health insurance*— . . . Last year when my car broke down, and I had to walk through the snow to get your groceries—

CHARLIE: I offered to get your car fixed—

LIZ: And I refused because I thought you had seven hundred dollars in your bank account. *(Pause)* You had all that money that you were keeping a *secret* from me? Why were you doing that? What, you think I would try and *take* it from you?

CHARLIE: No, of course not, I . . . It's for Ellie. It's always been for Ellie. *(Pause)* If there was ever some kind of emergency, I would have given you money—

LIZ: Would you? You've been keeping this from me for years, you really think I can trust you?

(Pause. Liz starts grabbing her things.)

CHARLIE: Please don't go.

(Liz exits. Pause.)

ELLIE: Mom—you're not getting any of my money.

MARY: Oh, shut up, Ellie. *(Pause)* Both of you, leave. Right now.

(Pause.)

ELLIE: I need the car keys.
MARY: You can walk.
ELLIE: It's like two miles!
MARY: Do you really think that I care?
ELLIE: I hate you.

(Ellie exits. Elder Thomas moves out of the corner, moving toward Charlie.)

ELDER THOMAS: I'll come back.

(Charlie looks at him.
Elder Thomas exits. A long moment of silence.
Mary stares at Charlie. She stands up, still looking at him.
She circles his wheelchair, looking at him from all sides.)

MARY: Jesus, Charlie.

(Pause. Mary looks away. She takes a cigarette out of her purse, lights it up.)

So this—heart thing. It's serious, yeah?
CHARLIE: Pretty serious.
MARY: You gonna be okay?

(Pause.)

CHARLIE: I'll be fine.

(Pause.)

MARY: Do you have anything?

CHARLIE: What? *(Pause)* Oh, uh—maybe, in the kitchen. There might be something in the cabinet over the stove, the highest shelf on the right.

(Mary exits momentarily, returning with a bottle of vodka and a glass. She pours a large drink for herself, drinks.)

MARY: Our deal was we'd wait until she was out of the house to give her the money.

CHARLIE: What's the difference?

MARY: The difference is she's seventeen and in high school. She's going to spend it on ponies or marijuana or something.

CHARLIE: I think she's a little smarter than that.

MARY: I really wish you wouldn't have done this, Charlie. This is the last thing I need right now. *(Taking a long drink)* How has it been? Getting to know her.

CHARLIE: She's—amazing.

(Mary chuckles.)

MARY: You still do that.

CHARLIE: What?

MARY: That positivity. It's so annoying.

CHARLIE *(Smiling)*: Well, you're a complete cynic, I was just trying to balance us out.

MARY: I guess I do miss that. That one thing.

CHARLIE: Just that?

MARY: That, and the cooking. Last month I tried to make a pie and I nearly set the entire apartment building on fire, Ellie threw all our pots and pans into the dumpster so I'd never try to do it again. You still cook?

CHARLIE: Not for years now. It's—hard for me to get into the kitchen.

(Pause.)

MARY: Charlie, I . . . I never knew you were doing this to yourself.

CHARLIE: You never asked me how I was doing.

MARY: You never asked me how I was doing either. Every month it's just, "How much money do you need?" And, "How's Ellie?"

CHARLIE: You didn't tell me she was failing out of high school.

MARY: Well, now you know. I guess I just didn't need the lecture from you about my involvement in her education.

CHARLIE: That's not what I—

(Long pause.)

How are you doing, Mary?

(Pause.)

MARY: Fine.

CHARLIE: Are you working?

MARY: No.

CHARLIE: Do you need me to send more money?

MARY: *No.*

(Pause.)

CHARLIE: It's good to see you. *(Pause)* Mary, I know that I screwed everything up. I know it must have been terrible. And humiliating. And I know that I'm not supposed to be around her—hell, you could call the police if you want to—

MARY: Christ, you really think I'd do that?

CHARLIE: You fought me pretty hard for full custody. And I don't blame you, after what I did. But I just want to see her—I've *always* just wanted to see her. Is it so awful that she has a gay father?

MARY: No, actually, it's not. *(Pause)* She's—awful, isn't she?

CHARLIE: What?

MARY: Ellie. She's awful. She's a terror.

CHARLIE: No, she's—she has a strong personality, but—

MARY: Charlie, she doesn't even have any *friends*. Not a single one. She's so cruel that no one at school will even *talk* to her. *(Pause)* When she was nine, ten, I thought—I'm not giving him the satisfaction. I'm not letting him see this awful little girl and blame it all on me. No way.

CHARLIE: Wait, is that why you've been keeping her from me all this time? You thought I would think you were a bad mother?

MARY: At first. But later on—when she was fifteen, sixteen. I was worried she would hurt you.

CHARLIE: "Hurt" me? That's ridiculous—

MARY: You've been around her for two days now, and already she's almost killed you. *(Pause)* I was protecting you, Charlie. You've always been so fucking sensitive, ready to break down over anything . . . And here's this girl—this girl who takes *pleasure* in hurting people, this *terrible* girl. *(Pause)* Believe me, Charlie, I don't take any pleasure in admitting it, I'm her mother for Christ's sake. I spent way too many years saying to myself, She's just rebellious, she's just difficult. Charlie—she's evil.

CHARLIE: *She is not evil.*

(Pause. Mary goes to Charlie's laptop, types.)

What are you doing?

MARY: Just—.

CHARLIE: If you're gonna show me Ellie's site, I've already seen it—

MARY: Did you see what she posted this morning?

(Mary brings the laptop to Charlie. Charlie looks at the screen.)

When I saw this picture of you . . . I thought I should come over.

(Charlie continues looking at the laptop.)

CHARLIE *(Reading)*: "There'll be a grease fire in Hell when he starts to burn."

(Pause.)

MARY: Don't feel bad, I've made quite a few appearances on that little site of hers. *(Pause)* You okay?

(Pause.)

CHARLIE: She's a strong writer.
MARY: *That's* your response?
CHARLIE: This isn't evil, this is honesty. Do you know how much bullshit I've read in my life?
MARY: My God, things never change. I don't understand you, Charlie.
CHARLIE: Every time I called you, I'd ask about her and you'd tell me she was doing fine. If she's so evil, why didn't you ever—
MARY: What was I supposed to tell you? That she was off treating her friends like dirt and slashing her teachers' tires? You didn't want to hear about that stuff.
CHARLIE: I could have helped her!
MARY: She doesn't want your help! She doesn't want anyone!

(Mary gets up, wandering aimlessly around the room, drunk by this point and a little shaky on her feet.)

CHARLIE: Mary, sit down.

MARY: You think I didn't want her to have a dad? She *adored* you. The only reason you married me in the first place was to have a kid, I know that.

CHARLIE: *Mary. Please.*

(Mary stops, gets her drink and sits down.)

MARY: This brings back memories, doesn't it? *(Pause)* Listen. I . . . I never got to say that I was sorry.

CHARLIE: What would you have to be sorry about?

MARY: That's not what I mean, I . . . I mean about your—friend.

CHARLIE: Oh. *(Pause)* His name was Alan.

MARY: I know his fucking name, Charlie. *(Pause)* I saw him once, after you left. In the Kmart parking lot. I should have wanted to run him over, or punch him in the face, but when I went up to him, he was so— . . . He was carrying these bags, he could barely lift them, he was so thin. Looked like he was about to fall over. I went up to him with all these amazing things I was going to say, hurl at him like bricks. And I looked at him, and I—asked him if he wanted some help. He let me carry a couple of bags to his car for him, he said thank you, and I left. I never even told him who I was. *(Pause)* When I heard what happened, I thought about coming by. Bringing Ellie to see you. I should have done that, I guess, and I'm sorry.

CHARLIE: It's okay. I'd be angry at me too. *(Pause)* But thank you. For saying that.

(Pause.)

MARY: You're wheezing.

CHARLIE: Yeah. It's gotten worse.

MARY: Are you having trouble breathing? Should I call someone?

CHARLIE: No, it's—
MARY: Let me hear.

(Mary puts her ear to Charlie's chest, listening to him breathe.)

CHARLIE: How do I sound?

(No response.)

Today was the first time we were all together in fifteen years, you realize that? *(Pause)* Back when Ellie was first born, we did that road trip to the Oregon coast together. And we stayed in Newport, and Ellie loved the sand so much. You and I laid on the beach together, and Ellie played in the surf, and later that day I went swimming in the ocean. Last time I ever went swimming, actually. And I kept cutting my legs on the rocks, and the water was so cold, and you were so mad that my legs bled and stained the seats in the minivan. And you said for days after that I smelled like seawater. You remember that?

(Charlie puts his hand on Mary's back as she listens. Silence.)

MARY: You sound awful.
CHARLIE: I'm dying, Mary.

(Mary looks at him.)

MARY: Fuck you.
CHARLIE: I'm sorry.
MARY: *Fuck you. (Pause)* For sure?
CHARLIE: Yeah. For sure. *(Pause)* Listen to me. I need to make certain that Ellie's going to be okay. Beyond the money. She has to have someone around who won't give up on her.

(Pause.)

MARY: You've been eating yourself to death for fifteen years and you're saying that *I* gave up on her?

CHARLIE: I wanted to see her, Mary, I wanted to be a part of her life—both of your lives—

MARY: Go to the hospital, Charlie! You have money, go to the hospital!

CHARLIE: We both know that money is for Ellie. But beyond that, I have to make sure that she's going to be all right, I have to be sure that she's going to have a decent life, where people care for her and she cares for other people— . . . She doesn't have anyone else, Mary.

MARY *(Grabbing her things)*: I have to . . . I need to go.

CHARLIE: I need to know I did *one thing* right in my life.

(Mary heads to the door. She opens the door and then stops, not looking at Charlie.)

MARY: We both did our parts. I raised her, you're giving her the money. It's the best we could do. *(Pause, still not looking at him)* Do you need anything before I leave? Water, or something?

(Pause.)

CHARLIE: No.

(Pause.)

MARY: Do you— . . . Do you want me to help you to the bathroom?

(Charlie doesn't respond. Mary waits for a beat, then exits.)

NIGHT

Charlie is asleep in his wheelchair. His wheezing has gotten much worse, and his breathing is shallow enough that it starts to affect his speech; he often has to pause mid-sentence to take a breath.

There is a loud knock at the door, Charlie wakes up with a start, the sudden movement producing pain in his chest. He winces. Another loud knock.

CHARLIE: Liz?

ELDER THOMAS *(Offstage)*: Can I come inside?

CHARLIE: What the hell are you—? Are you okay?

ELDER THOMAS *(Offstage)*: I'm fine, please let me come inside!

CHARLIE: Yes, just—!

(Elder Thomas enters.)

Are you—? What's wrong?

ELDER THOMAS: I'm sorry, I'm really, really, really high.

CHARLIE: Why are you high?

ELDER THOMAS: My parents called me tonight.

CHARLIE: So?

ELDER THOMAS: My parents found out where I am. They found out that I'm in Idaho.

CHARLIE: I don't understand.

ELDER THOMAS: Your daughter, she sent pictures of me smoking pot to the mission in Oregon, and told them where I was. And my parents saw the pictures, and they called the church here in town, and they told them where I was staying, and I can't figure out if she was trying to help me or hurt me. Do you ever get that feeling with her?

CHARLIE: I don't. Really understand—

ELDER THOMAS: I thought my parents were going to disown me, and you know what they said? They said they *loved* me, they *cared* about me, and they wanted me to come home. How *awful* is that?

(Charlie feels a sharp pain in his chest, he bends his head down in pain.)

What's wrong?

CHARLIE: I'm fine.

ELDER THOMAS: No, you're not.

CHARLIE: It's just . . . It's going to go away, it just hurts—

ELDER THOMAS: I just want to help. I know I can help you.

CHARLIE: I'm not going to the hospital—

ELDER THOMAS: I know. I won't make you go. But I can help you.

CHARLIE: Look, just go home to your family, if you need money for a bus or something—

ELDER THOMAS: I know what happened to Alan.

(Pause.)

CHARLIE: What?

ELDER THOMAS: I know what happened that day, at church, the last time he was there. *(Pause)* I got an e-mail tonight,

87

from Cindy Miller, from the church. She remembers.
I had to come tell you right away.

(Silence.)

CHARLIE: What did they do to him?

(Short pause.)

ELDER THOMAS: The talk that day, the talk that his father gave—
it was about *Jonah*.

(Pause.)

CHARLIE: What?

ELDER THOMAS: *Jonah and the whale. (Pause)* Don't you see?
That essay you had me read to you—the one you like so
much, the one about *Moby Dick* . . . Charlie, I get it now,
I understand what God's been doing with me here,
I understand why he sent me to you, right when you
needed help. This isn't just a coincidence, when I read
that e-mail—I knew I was helping you talk with God. It
reaffirmed my faith. *(Pause)* Jonah—it's about refusing the
call of God, you know? Jonah tries to escape from God's
will, he gets swallowed by a whale, and when he prays to
God for help, God saves him by making the whale spit
him out onto shore.

(Silence.

Charlie laughs a little bit, the laughter causing pain in his
chest.)

CHARLIE: Is this what it fucking comes down to? I always
thought, whatever they did to him that day must have
been so awful, so cruel . . . A story? Some stupid *story*,
that's what killed him?

ELDER THOMAS: No, it's *not* just a story—

CHARLIE: Look, I appreciate what you're trying to do, but this doesn't mean anything, it—. I don't even know what I was expecting to find out, it's not—

ELDER THOMAS: *Listen to me. (Short pause)* Charlie, your boyfriend—he tried to escape God's will, he chose his lifestyle with you over God. And when he heard this story, when he heard *God's word*, he knew. He knew the *truth*. He never prayed for salvation—but it's not too late for you.

(Pause.)

CHARLIE: You think Alan died—because he chose to be with me? You think God turned his back on him because he and I were in love?

ELDER THOMAS: *Yes.*

(Silence. Charlie stares at him.)

CHARLIE: You know, I wasn't always this big.

(Short pause.)

ELDER THOMAS: Yeah, I know—

CHARLIE: I mean, I was never the best-looking guy in the room, but—Alan still loved me. He still thought I was beautiful.

ELDER THOMAS: Okay—

CHARLIE: Halfway through the semester, he started meeting me during my office hours—we were both crazy about one another, but we waited until the course was done before we . . .

ELDER THOMAS: This isn't important—

CHARLIE: It was just after classes had ended for the year, it was a perfect temperature, and we went for a walk in the arboretum. And we kissed.

ELDER THOMAS: Charlie, stop.

CHARLIE: Listen to me. We used to spend entire nights lying next to one another, naked—

ELDER THOMAS: Stop.

CHARLIE: We would make love—

ELDER THOMAS: I don't want to hear about—

CHARLIE: *We would make love.* Do you find that disgusting?

ELDER THOMAS: Charlie, God is ready to help you, you don't have to—

CHARLIE: *I hope there isn't a God. (Pause)* I hope there isn't a God because I hate thinking that there's an afterlife, that Alan can see what I've done to myself, that he can see my swollen feet, the sores on my skin, the patches of mold in between the flaps—

ELDER THOMAS: Okay, *stop—*

CHARLIE: —the infected ulcers on my ass, the sack of fat on my back that turned brown last year—

ELDER THOMAS: *Stop*

CHARLIE: This is disgusting?

ELDER THOMAS: YES.

CHARLIE: *I'm* disgusting?

ELDER THOMAS: YES, YOU'RE DISGUSTING, YOU'RE— ...

(Elder Thomas stops himself.
Long silence. Charlie stares at him.)

CHARLIE: Go home to your family.

(Pause. Elder Thomas exits. Charlie breathes heavily, wheezing, trying to calm himself down.
The lights quickly snap to black.
In the darkness, the waves are heard once again—this time definite, sharp and aggressive, rising quickly in volume until lights rise on:)

Friday

Charlie, at his laptop, speaking into a microphone. A small webcam rests next to his laptop, not hooked up. Charlie is noticeably weaker, and is having trouble maintaining his line of thought.

CHARLIE: So, here we are. Your complaints have been heard. The powers that be have decided to replace me with someone else—someone more "stable" and "traditional" as the e-mail to me said. This person will no doubt make you rewrite and rewrite and rewrite, just like I did for seventeen years, analyzing every word, every punctuation mark for clarity and precision of meaning, and . . . *(Pause)* You all sent me your essays. Your new essays, the ones you didn't rewrite. The ones you didn't think about, and . . .

(Charlie types for a second, pulling up something on his laptop.)

KristyStar9, you wrote: "My parents want me to be a radiologist, but I don't even know what that is." Peter6969, you wrote: "I'm sick of people telling me that I have promise." AdamD567, about two pages in, you wrote: "I think I need to accept that my life isn't going to be very exciting." You all wrote these—*amazing*, things, I just— *(Pause)* I want to be honest with you now. I've been just a voice to all of you all semester, and now you've been so honest with me, I just . . .

(Charlie pauses, then plugs the webcam into his laptop. He stares at it for a second. He moves the camera away from him, then tilts it down, filming his body. He brings the camera back up to his face.)

These assignments—they don't matter. This course doesn't matter. College doesn't matter. These beautiful, honest things you wrote—they matter.

(Charlie pauses a second, then throws the laptop and camera across the room. They crash against the wall.)

Charlie is sitting in his wheelchair. Liz stands in the doorway, staring at the broken laptop, holding her bag.

CHARLIE: I'm sorry.
LIZ: Don't.

> *(Liz makes her way inside, closes the door slowly. She moves over to Charlie.)*

CHARLIE: Liz—
LIZ: I said don't.

> *(Liz stares at him for a second. She reaches into her bag, pulling out a stethoscope. She puts it on, then moves toward Charlie, putting it on his chest. She gently adjusts the oxygen tube underneath his nose.)*

Breathe in.

(Charlie breathes in.)

More.

CHARLIE: I can't. Hurts.

(Liz takes the stethoscope off, puts it back in her bag. She looks at Charlie.)

LIZ: I really hate you for putting me through this again, you know that? *(Pause)* Those last few months before Alan . . . And I'd come over here, and I'd scream at him, shake him, *for God's sake, eat something . . . (Pause)* I'd come back and the food would be gone. Not because he ate it—but because he hid it somewhere. Threw it out the window, fed it to the neighbor's dog. You were beside yourself, had no idea what to do . . . God, that was awful.

CHARLIE: It was awful for me, too.

LIZ: Well, you weren't the one who found him. In your bed, underneath the covers, curled up like a fetus. God, you think you only see things like that in documentaries.

(Liz reaches into her bag, taking out two sub sandwiches.)

I got you two meatball subs. Extra cheese. I don't know what I'm doing. *(Pause)* You have money. You need to go to the hospital.

(Pause.)

CHARLIE: No.

LIZ: For me. Go to the hospital for me.

CHARLIE: No.

(Pause.)

LIZ: How *dare* you do this to me again?!

(Silence. Charlie's breathing is increasingly shallow.
The sound of waves is heard at a very low level, steadily
increasing in volume as the scene progresses.)

CHARLIE: She helped him.

LIZ: What?

CHARLIE: She wasn't trying to hurt him. She was trying to help
him.

LIZ: Who are you talking about?

CHARLIE: The Mormon kid. He's going home. She did that.
She wasn't trying to hurt him.

LIZ: Oh, God, Charlie?

CHARLIE: She didn't do it to hurt him, she did it to send him
home.

LIZ: Do you feel light-headed? Charlie, look at me.

CHARLIE: She was trying to help him!

LIZ: Who?!

CHARLIE: Ellie. She was trying to help him, she just wanted
him to go home.

LIZ: Oh my God. You need—. I don't know what to do, I can't
help you!

(Charlie looks at Liz.)

CHARLIE: Do you ever get the feeling. That people. Are incapable. Of not caring? People. Are. Amazing.

(Ellie charges in through the front door holding the essay from
before. She stops when she sees Charlie, looking at him for a
brief moment.)

ELLIE: What's wrong with him?

LIZ: He's dying.

(Pause.)

ELLIE: So call someone.
CHARLIE: No.
ELLIE: Call an ambulance.
CHARLIE: No. Liz. Please don't.
ELLIE: Call a fucking ambulance!

(Liz takes out her cell phone.)

CHARLIE: Liz. Please.
LIZ: No. I'm not letting this go on anymore, I'm calling an ambulance. I'm not going through this again!
ELLIE: I need to talk to him.

(Liz starts dialing.)

LIZ: So talk.
ELLIE: Alone.
LIZ: I'm not leaving you alone with him.
ELLIE: I need to talk to him alone!
CHARLIE: Liz. Please.

(Liz looks at him. Pause.)

LIZ: Fine. I'm calling an ambulance, and I'm waiting down-stairs. We'll get you to the hospital, and you're *going to be fine.* You understand me?

(Liz exits.)

ELLIE: What's wrong with you?
CHARLIE: I can't. Breathe very well.

(Pause.)

ELLIE: The ambulance is coming. They'll take you to the hospital, you should have gone a while ago. *(Pause)* Why did you do that?!

CHARLIE: What?

(Ellie holds up the essay.)

ELLIE: I failed.

CHARLIE: It's. A really good essay.

ELLIE: No, it's not a really good essay! I failed! *(Pause)* Are you just trying to screw me over one last time before you die? I don't care that you're dying! I don't care about you! Do you want me to fail out of high school, is that why you did this?

CHARLIE: I didn't. Write it.

ELLIE: This is the essay you gave me yesterday.

CHARLIE: You didn't. Read it.

ELLIE: I don't need to read it, it got an F!

CHARLIE: Read it.

(Ellie looks at the paper for a second.)

ELLIE: This is . . . I know what this is.

CHARLIE: I knew you would. You never. Forget anything.

ELLIE: I wrote this. *(Pause)* I wrote this in eighth grade for English, why do you—?

CHARLIE: "And I felt saddest of all. When I read the boring chapters. That were only descriptions of whales. Because I knew. That the author was just trying to save us. From his own sad story. Just for a little while."

ELLIE: Why do you have this?

CHARLIE: Your mother. She sent it to me. Four years ago. I wanted to know how you were doing. In school. So she sent it. And it's the best essay. I've ever read.

(Pause.)

ELLIE: Why are you fucking with me like this?

CHARLIE: I'm not. *(Pause)* You're so beautiful. Ellie, you're beautiful.

ELLIE: Stop saying that.

CHARLIE: You're amazing. This essay. Is amazing.

ELLIE: Stop saying that!

CHARLIE: You're the best thing. I've ever done.

(Charlie has a severe chest pain, he doubles over. Ellie is frantic.)

ELLIE: What's the matter?!

CHARLIE: Ellie.

ELLIE: I can't be here right now, I have to go, I can't—

CHARLIE: You're perfect. You'll be happy. You'll care for people.

ELLIE: The ambulance is coming, they'll help you!

CHARLIE: No. They won't.

(Pause.)

ELLIE: *You're going to the hospital.*

CHARLIE: No.

ELLIE: You just need surgery or something!

CHARLIE: Read it to me.

ELLIE: What?!

CHARLIE: If you want to help. Read it to me. You can help me. If you read it.

(Ellie is holding back tears at this point.)

ELLIE: You asshole. You fat fucking asshole!

CHARLIE: You'll help. If you read it.

ELLIE: Fuck you.

CHARLIE: Please.

ELLIE: Fuck you!

CHARLIE: Ellie.

ELLIE: Dad, *please.*

(Pause. Ellie looks at Charlie, pleading. Ellie and Charlie are in almost the same position as they were at the end of their first scene together. The sound of waves gets louder and louder.)

(Reading) "In the amazing book *Moby Dick* by the author Herman Melville, the author recounts his story of being at sea. In the first part of his book, the author, calling himself Ishmael, is in a small seaside town and he is sharing a bed with a man named Queequeg."

(Charlie smiles at Ellie through the pain. He reaches up and takes the oxygen tube out of his nose.)

"The author and Queequeg go to church and hear a sermon about Jonah, and later set out on a ship captained by the pirate named Ahab, who is missing a leg, and very much wants to kill the whale which is named Moby Dick, and which is white."

(Charlie braces himself on his wheelchair.)

"In the course of the book, the pirate Ahab encounters many hardships. His entire life is set around trying to kill a certain whale."

(Wheezing heavily, and with a huge amount of effort and pain, Charlie manages to stand up.)

"I think this is sad because this whale doesn't have any emotions, and doesn't know how bad Ahab wants to kill him."

(Charlie, staring at Ellie, manages to take one step forward. His breathing becomes quicker. The waves are louder still.)

"He's just a poor big animal. And I feel bad for Ahab as well, because he thinks that his life will be better if he can kill this whale, but in reality it won't help him at all."

(Charlie takes another step. His breathing is more and more rapid.)

"I was very saddened by this book, and I felt many emotions for the characters."

(Another step.)

"And I felt saddest of all when I read the boring chapters that were only descriptions of whales, because I knew that the author was just trying to save us from his own sad story, just for a little while."

(Charlie takes one last step toward Ellie. The waves reach their loudest level.)

"This book made me think about my own life, and then it made me feel glad for my—"

*(Charlie looks up. The waves cut off.
A sharp intake of breath. The lights snap to black.)*

END OF PLAY

A Bright New Boise

PRODUCTION HISTORY

A Bright New Boise was commissioned and first produced by Partial Comfort Productions (Chad Beckim and Molly Pearson, Co-Artistic Directors), and received its world premiere at the Wild Project in New York City, on September 15, 2010. It was directed by Davis McCallum. The set design was by Jason Simms, the costume design was by Whitney Locher, the lighting design was by Raquel Davis, the original music was by Ryan Rumery and the video design was by Rocco D'Santi; the production stage manager was Tara Nachtigall. The cast was:

WILL	Andrew Garman
PAULINE	Danielle Slavick
ANNA	Sarah Nina Hayon
LEROY	John Patrick Doherty
ALEX	Matt Farabee

A Bright New Boise opened at the Woolly Mammoth Theatre Company (Howard Shalwitz, Artistic Director; Jeffrey Herrmann, Managing Director) in Washington, DC, on October 10, 2011. It was directed by John Vreeke. The set design was by Misha Kachman, the costume design was by Ivania Stack, the lighting design was by Colin K. Bills, the sound design and original music were by Chris Baine and the video design was by Aaron Fisher; the production stage manager was William E. Cruttenden III. The cast was:

WILL	Michael Russotto
PAULINE	Emily Townley
ANNA	Kimberly Gilbert
LEROY	Felipe Cabezas
ALEX	Joshua Morgan
MEN ON TV	Michael Glenn and Michael Willis

Characters

WILL	Male, late thirties
PAULINE	Female, late thirties to early forties
ANNA	Female, late twenties to early thirties
LEROY	Male, early to mid-twenties
ALEX	Male, seventeen
TWO MALE VOICES ON HOBBY LOBBY TV	

Setting

Aside from the scenes in the parking lot, the entire play takes place in a windowless break room of a Hobby Lobby in Boise, Idaho. Stark, fluorescent lighting, white walls. A few cheap chairs and tables are in the space, along with a telephone on the wall, an ethernet port, lockers, a mounted TV, maybe a vending machine or mini-fridge. Some non-ironic corporate slogans or work schedules adorning the walls wouldn't be out of order.

Notes

"Hobby Lobby TV" should be a recording of two men sitting behind a desk, with a very dull background, either completely unadorned or with a very cheap-looking "Hobby Lobby" sign behind them. It should always be at an extremely low, barely perceptible volume (except when indicated), and the dialogue should be as plain, boring and nondescript as possible. No effort should be made to make it funny, ironic, meaningful, etc. It should only be slow, low-pitched, monotonous chatter about new items, sales and promotions, new store locations, etc.

In production, the TV can be handled in a number of different ways. In the first production, the TV was almost entirely facing upstage so that the audience never saw the images. In the second production, the TV was visible at all times and actors portrayed the voices.

Dialogue written in *italics* is emphatic, deliberate; dialogue in ALL CAPS is impulsive, explosive.

A " / " indicates an overlap in dialogue.

An intermission can be taken between scenes six and seven.

Scene 1

Will stands in a parking lot, at night.

Sounds of an interstate can be heard: passing semis, car horns, car stereos, etc., as well as the buzzing glow of neon signs and fluorescent lights overhead.

Awash in the light, he stands with his eyes closed, listening to the noise.

WILL: Now.

. . .

. . .

. . .

Now.

. . .

. . .

. . .

Now.

. . .

. . .

. . .

Now.

(The noise continues.)

Scene 2

The break room. Will sits facing Pauline, whose back is to the TV.
Pauline wears a nametag and holds a clipboard.
An extreme close-up of ear surgery plays on the TV.

PAULINE: So then the black guy comes up to the Asian lady
and the white lady, and he's like, "I don't really understand
what all this talk about unions is gonna get us. All they
wanna do is take our money and decide who we're going
to vote for." And then the Asian lady is like, *shocked*, and
she says, "They choose who you vote for?" And then the
white lady says, "That's not what America is all about." And
then there's a graphic, or . . . Shit, what the hell is . . . ? It's
like a pie chart. Yeah, it's like—I don't know, something
about unions. Do you know anything about unions?

WILL: They're not good.

PAULINE: Yeah, exactly. That's the gist of the pie chart, anyway,
so you get it. Sorry you couldn't just watch it, the damn

VCR's broken. Everything here is falling apart, including me. Heh, you know.

will: Oh. Yeah, heh.

pauline: So anyway, don't try to unionize.

will: Oh, no, of course not.

pauline: They shut down a Hobby Lobby in Kansas City when they tried to unionize, so don't try to unionize.

will: I really won't.

pauline: Too bad you couldn't see the video, it's actually—it has a funny segment, like a cartoon?

will: Oh, okay.

pauline: Yeah, it's actually a pretty great company when it comes down to it. And they know how to run a business, everything is hooked up to the corporate office. We can't even turn the air-conditioning on without calling Oklahoma. I mean—I know that sounds annoying, but it's actually really great. Really, it's just—a well-oiled machine.

will: Yeah, I'm really glad you had an open position—

pauline *(Holding Will's résumé)*: Says here you worked for Albertsons up in Coeur d'Alene?

will: Uh—yes.

pauline: Uh-huh. And how was that?

will: Oh, it was—fine, I guess.

pauline: I used to be assistant manager at Fred Meyer, you know Fred Meyer?

will: Oh yeah, of course.

pauline: It's kind of like an Albertsons.

(Quick pause.)

will: Y—yes.

(Pauline continues to look through his résumé.)

pauline: You from Coeur d'Alene originally?

WILL: The area, yeah.

PAULINE: Beautiful up there.

WILL: Yes, it really is.

PAULINE: What brings you down to Boise?

WILL: I guess—change in scenery more than anything else.

PAULINE: Yeah? Well, Boise's a good town. You'll like it here, it's grown a lot over the past ten years.

WILL: Yes, it really / seems like—

PAULINE: When I was a kid, it was nothing like this. Where we're sitting right now used to be cow pastures. Nowadays, all the surrounding towns just spill right into one another. Friend of mine lives in Caldwell, tells me sometimes it takes him *forty minutes* to get to work. We have honest-to-god *city traffic*, you believe that?

WILL: Yeah, I haven't been here since I was a kid, it's much different—

PAULINE *(Looking at the résumé)*: Why'd you switch to part-time in 2004?

(Pause.)

WILL: What's that?

PAULINE: At Albertsons. You switched to part-time in 2004, how come?

WILL: Oh, I had a—sort of a second job.

PAULINE: What was it?

WILL: Uh—I was, it was sort of like, uh—bookkeeping?

PAULINE: Why isn't it on your résumé?

WILL: Well, it wasn't really . . . It was very specific, it was for a church.

PAULINE: So?

WILL: Oh, you just . . . I don't know, sometimes people—they make assumptions about who you are based on—

PAULINE: Hell, we're not like that, believe me. The guy who founded the company is all, like, Christian. David Green, that's the guy's name. You should read the statement of purpose for the company, it's all like—

WILL: Plus, all my other experience is in retail, I thought that was more important.

PAULINE: Huh. Well, anyway, I can get you started as soon as you like. Tomorrow, even. Pays $7.25 an hour, I'll try to put you on full-time in nine months if I can, until then you work thirty-eight hours a week. Holidays are time and a half, weekends are time and a quarter. Possible seventy-cent raise after nine months.

WILL: Perfect.

PAULINE: All right then. I'll go get your W-2. Do you have your social security card and driver's license on you? I can take you out on the floor and we can get going on your training. I'll set up an appointment for the drug test for tomorrow morning. You have any questions?

WILL: Yeah, just—is that always on the TV in here?

(Pauline turns around, sees the TV.)

PAULINE: Goddammit. Motherfucker. Goddammit.

(Pauline gets up and goes to the TV, looking at it.)

Goddammit. What is that, an ear? That's an ear, isn't it? Goddammit.

(Pauline picks up the phone and dials a few numbers.)

(On the phone) Leroy, go up to the roof and—. Yeah, it's an ear or something. *(Hangs up)*
    Sorry about that. Goddammit.

WILL: Why is—?

PAULINE: It's the satellite dish, I don't know. Sometimes it gets all screwy, is it raining outside?

WILL: A little bit, yeah.

PAULINE: Figures. The company has its own dedicated channel—nothing much, just info on products, new stores, stuff like that. Sometimes the signal gets crossed with these medical whatevers.

(*Looking at the TV*) Goddamn, would you look at that? How do you think that feels? Jesus Christ.

(*Will cringes. Pauline notices.*)

Don't worry, you'll get used to it. You're not gonna vomit, are you? Interviewed a girl last month, she almost threw up. I didn't hire her.

WILL: I'm fine, it's fine.

(*Alex enters, listening to his iPod. He doesn't look at either Pauline or Will and sits down on one of the chairs, facing away from them.*
  Will stares at Alex.)

PAULINE (*Regarding Alex*): He's twelve. Doesn't speak English so we can work him seventy hours a week.

WILL: What?

PAULINE: I'm shitting you, he's a high school kid. Worked here last summer too.

(*To Alex*) Hey. Hey, Alex. Say hi to Will! He's new!

(*No response.*)

ALEX FUCKING SAY HI TO WILL. MAKE HIM FEEL WELCOME.

(*Alex barely looks up, does a halfhearted wave toward Will. Will smiles, waves back.*)

Good worker, actually. Real accurate register counts.

ANNA *(Over the PA)*: Mandy, personal call on line two. Mandy, line two.
PAULINE: Fuckin' Mandy. *(Referring to social security card and driver's license)* Can I grab those to make a copy?

(No response.)

Will?
WILL: Uh—yeah, here.

(Will hands her his social security card and driver's license. Pauline exits. Will continues to stare at Alex. After a moment, Alex feels someone looking at him.
He looks behind him, seeing Will. Will smiles warmly at him. Alex smiles back, then goes back to his iPod.
He still feels Will staring at his back, he looks back at Will again.)

What're you listening to?
ALEX *(Taking off his headphones)*: What?
WILL: Sorry, I—I'm just wondering, what're you listening to?
ALEX: Villa-Lobos.

(Pause.)

WILL: Is that—pop music?
ALEX: He's a composer who mixed traditional Brazilian music with European classical music.
WILL: Oh. Wow. That's impressive.
ALEX: Yeah, well, I'm glad you're impressed, that means a lot.

(Alex looks away, putting his headphones back on. Will keeps looking at him. Finally, Alex looks at him.)

WILL *(Reaching out a hand)*: I'm Will. I just got hired.

(Alex takes off his headphones again.)

ALEX: Wait, you wanna like, talk?

(Pause.)

I'm Alex.

(Pause.)

WILL: What other kinds of music do you listen to?
ALEX: Lots. Mostly modern composition.
WILL: What does that mean?
ALEX: Like, composers. Who are modern.

(Pause.)

WILL: Are you a / musician?
ALEX: I'm gonna listen to my music now if that's okay.

(Alex smiles at him, putting his headphones back on. He turns on his iPod, scrolling through the music.)

WILL: Alex?

(Alex takes out one ear bud, annoyed.)

ALEX: Yeah?
WILL: I'm your father. When you were born your name was William. You were named after me.

(Pauline reenters.)

PAULINE: Okay, so here we are. If you can get these done fast, I should be able to train you on one of the registers before

115

we close. Should be quick, if you remember anything from Albertsons, you'll be able to pick it up pretty—

(With a burst of static, the TV flips back to Hobby Lobby TV. Alex hurries out of the room.)

Ah, there we go. These two guys, they never say their names on the air for some reason. Everybody has guesses of what their names are. I think they both sound like they're kinda high, so I call this one Woody and this one Harrelson. Get it?

(Pause.)

WILL: No, sorry, I don't.

Scene 3

Later that night, back in the break room. The room is dark except for the glow of the TV, still tuned to Hobby Lobby TV.

Anna enters, cautiously making her way into the room. She sits at a break room table and takes out a book, a book light and a plastic bag full of jerky. She opens the book and begins to munch on the jerky.

After a moment, Will enters holding a laptop, turning on the lights. Anna lets out a little scream and drops her book. Will, startled, lets out a little yell as well.

WILL: OH—
ANNA: I'm sorry. I'm sorry.

(Anna desperately starts grabbing her things.)

WILL: No, I'm sorry—
ANNA: I'm leaving, I'll leave. I'm sorry, I just— *(Quick pause)*
    I know this looks weird, but I was just reading, I wasn't

doing anything strange, I just . . . *(Pause)* Are you—? Wait, who are you?

WILL: I'm new, I just got hired today—

ANNA *(Relieved)*: Oh . . . My God, I thought you were from corporate. Oh my God.

WILL: Corporate?

ANNA: They send—the company, sometimes they send people from corporate to check out the store at night, after closing. Like, a surprise inspection.

WILL: Oh.

ANNA: They have a video about this, you didn't watch the video?

WILL: The—it was the VCR, it wasn't working.

(Pause.)

ANNA: Just—don't tell Pauline you saw me here after closing, okay?

WILL: As long as you don't tell her you saw me.

ANNA: Right. Ha, ha. *(Pause)* I'm sorry, so what are you—?

WILL *(Holding up the laptop)*: I don't have internet where I'm staying right now. I noticed the plug-in thing earlier. *(Pause)* Do you mind?

ANNA: No! No, I don't mind.

(Pause.)

WILL: So what are you—?

(Anna holds up her book, smiles awkwardly.)

You can't read at home?

(Anna gives him a look.)

Oh, sorry, I didn't mean—

ANNA: No, I can't read at home.
WILL: Oh.

(An awkward pause.
  Will hooks up his laptop to the ethernet jack, Anna goes back to reading. Will starts up his laptop, it chimes. Anna gives him a look. Will mouths, "Sorry." Pause.)

ANNA: I usually stick around until ten or eleven.
WILL: Oh.

(Another awkward pause. Anna goes back to reading. Will starts typing, hitting one key over and over. Anna gives him another look.
  After a moment, Will puts the laptop down, then goes to the TV, about to turn it off.)

ANNA: Could you—? I sort of like to keep it on.
WILL: Oh—
ANNA: I'd just—rather you didn't turn it off.
WILL: It's just, it's kind of—. Never mind, sorry.
ANNA: You know, I can read in my car, I can—
WILL: No, it's—you were here first, I'm sorry. *(Packing up)* I can come back later. How did—? How did you get back into the building?

(Pause.)

ANNA: Oh, I . . . It's silly. I just hide in the silk flower section right before closing. No one seems to notice when I don't leave with them, I don't know. It's stupid.

(Pause.)

Wait how did you get back in?

(Pause.)

WILL: Scrapbooking section.

(Short pause. They both start laughing, awkwardly at first.)

ANNA: Are you serious?
WILL: Yep.
ANNA: That's—that's just ridiculous, isn't it?
WILL: Yes, I guess it is.
ANNA: Pretty bold move on your first day.
WILL: I used to do it at the Albertsons I worked at all the time.
ANNA: Huh. And I thought I was the only wacko who did this.

(Anna smiles, walking toward Will and extending a hand.)

I'm Anna.
WILL: Will.
ANNA: Well hello, Will! *(A terrible attempt at a joke)* "Will" you be hiding—in the—

(Neither of them laugh. Anna looks away in shame for a moment, then recovers.)

If you don't mind, you know—we could both stay. I could read, and you could do your—work or whatever. Do you have a job online? That's so interesting. I'm talking too much, am I talking too much?
WILL: No, it's fine—it's not really a job. I mean, it doesn't pay anything. I have a . . .

(Pause.)

ANNA: What?
WILL: It's just so stupid, I . . . It's like—a blog. It's stupid, and I'm a big dork.

ANNA: That's not stupid! What are you talking about? A blog, that's so—hip. What kind of blog is it?

WILL *(Hesitating)*: Um. It's . . .

ANNA: What am I doing? Shut up, Anna.

WILL: No, it's—it's like a story. Like a long story, like—an online novel.

(Pause.)

ANNA: Holy crap, you write books?

WILL: Well—

ANNA: I love books! I read books all the time! You're actually a writer?!

WILL: I don't get paid or anything—

ANNA: So?! Holy crap! *(Pause)* Sorry, I just—you're a writer, that's so neat.

WILL: Well not lately. It's been kind of rough going.

ANNA: Writer's block?

WILL: Something like that. I keep forcing myself to sit down and write, but—nothing comes.

ANNA: Like a process. Like an artistic process, I get that, yep. *(Pause)* Well, I bet your book is great. A lot better than what I'm reading right here, I bet that much. What's your book about?

WILL: It's, uh—sort of like—Christian literature?

ANNA: Oh yeah? That's great! I read that one book, what's it called—*The Purpose Driven Life*. Yeah, that was good. Anyway, I'm a Christian, I've always believed in Jesus.

WILL: Yeah?

ANNA: Sure, what else is there to believe in?

(Will smiles. Pause.)

Are you sure you don't want me to leave?

will: It's fine, it's—actually nice to have some company. *(Pause)* If it's okay with you.

anna: Yes! It's. *(Pause)* Well, I'll let you work.

(Pause. Anna goes back to reading, smiles at him, then laughs a little.)

I'm sorry. I still just can't believe . . . Both of us hiding in here—

will: It's really pretty funny.

anna: It's so cute, I . . . *(Pause)* Okay. I read, you write.

will *(Smiling)*: Deal.

(Anna opens her book; Will opens his laptop.)

Scene 4

Early the next morning, in the parking lot. Will stands facing Alex.

WILL: Hi. *(Pause)* Thanks for meeting me. I think I rushed my introduction just a little bit, I didn't want to—scare you. *(Pause)* Did you tell your parents about me?

ALEX: No.

WILL: Okay. *(Pause)* I can't imagine what you're feeling right now, I can't imagine what you've thought about me all these years—

ALEX: I don't believe you.

(Silence. Will takes a step toward Alex, who backs away.)

WILL: I can tell you that you were born on May 22nd, that's your birthday, right? You have foster parents, their names are John and Cindy Erikson.

ALEX: Any idiot with access to Google could figure out all that.

(Pause.)

will: You have a birthmark on your lower back, on the right side. When you were little you had blond hair, but I guess it got darker as you grew up.

(Will pulls out his wallet, taking out a weathered photograph.)

That's you. At two months. That's me, holding you.

(Alex looks at the photograph, then hands it back to him.)

alex: Whatever, all babies look the same.

(Pause.)

will: Look, Alex, I can prove this to you if you need me to, I don't know how, but—
alex: How did you find me?
will: I tracked down John and Cindy years ago. They didn't want me to have any contact with you, but every year they send me a letter. About you. Like a—status report, I guess.
alex: Do you know John and Cindy?
will: No, I mean—not really—
alex: Yeah, well, they're assholes. If you are my father, then fuck you, because you gave me to assholes.
will: Oh. *(Pause)* Alex, I just want you to know that I didn't want to give you up. When your mother—
alex: Stop. *(Pause)* When I was little I used to have fantasies about my real dad coming to get me. Like he was a prisoner of war, or an FBI guy or something. He didn't work at the Hobby Lobby, that's for sure. Do you at least drive a cool car or live in a big house?
will: It's a '94 Subaru. And right now, it's also my house.
alex: I'm gonna kill myself.

WILL: What?

ALEX: Nothing, it's just something I say. So if you're really my father—*if*—what do you want from me? You better not need a kidney or something.

WILL: No, I don't, I . . . I just want to get to know you.

ALEX: Okay, but why now?

(Pause.)

WILL: Look, Alex, things in my life have sort of been turned upside down, and I've had to reconsider a lot of the decisions I've made, the things I believe in . . . I just want to make a fresh start.

ALEX: Huh. Well, good for you. *(Pause)* I have panic attacks. Sometimes more than once a week. Do you know what a panic attack is?

WILL: Yeah—

ALEX: No, you don't. You think that you might, but you don't. You probably think that it's just about me being stressed out, you think that I have a panic attack when I get a bad grade on a test or something. I get panic attacks over nothing. Absolutely nothing. I'll be at work, or at home, or at school, and suddenly I'll start shaking and I won't be able to breathe. *(Pause)* School counselor says that it might be a chemical imbalance. Or, she says, it might have something to do with my past. I think it has something to do with my past, so if you're my father, it's probably your fault.

(Pause.)

WILL: Maybe just lunch / sometime?

ALEX: I want a blood test.

(Pause.)

will: Okay. I can—I'm not really sure where to go, but I can find out, I can make some calls—

alex: Valley Medical Clinic. It's in Meridian, on 17th Street. I have an appointment for six, you have an appointment for seven. We're going separately, and you're paying for it. It's not cheap.

(Pause.)

will: Okay.

alex: And you need to know that if it turns out that you're my biological father, that doesn't necessarily mean anything. It doesn't mean I have to talk with you or interact with you in any way.

(Pause.)

will: Did you know that your real name is William?

alex: My real name isn't William.

will: It was the name your mother gave you when you were born.

alex: Don't ever call me William. If you call me William, I'm gonna kill myself.

will: I won't. I'm sorry.

alex: And don't talk about my mom unless I tell you to.

(Pause.)

will: I listened to some Villa-Lobos last night. Downloaded some albums.

alex: You did?

will: Yeah. Backa—?

alex: *Bachianas Brasileiras.*

will: Yeah.

alex: What did you think?

WILL: It was really pretty.

(Pause.)

ALEX: "Pretty"?
WILL: Yeah, and—
ALEX *(Under his breath)*: I'm gonna kill myself . . .
WILL: Overwhelming.

(Pause. Alex looks at him.)

ALEX: If I ask you to quit and move out of Boise, would you?

(Will doesn't answer, staring down at his shoes.)

I gotta clock in.

(Alex exits.)

Scene 5

Later that day. Leroy sits in the break room reading a newspaper, wearing a T-shirt that reads simply "FUCK" in large block letters. The TV is off. After a moment, Will enters with a Chef Boyardee microwaveable lunch. He notices Leroy's shirt, and nods politely at him.

Will goes to the microwave, puts in his lunch.

LEROY: It's a piece of shit.

WILL *(Turning)*: What's that?

LEROY: The microwave. It barely works. I'd recommend cranking it up to high and leaving it in there for at least three times longer than normal.

WILL: Oh—okay, thanks.

(Will turns the microwave on. It sputters to life, making intermittent noises that seem to suggest it's on its last leg.)

LEROY: How's the first day?

WILL: Second, actually. Well, first full day. It's—fine. Slow.

LEROY: It's always like this. You'd think they were losing money, but the profit margin is pretty amazing.

WILL: What do you mean?

LEROY: Think about it. They're just selling all this raw material: fabric, paint, balsa wood, whatever. It's like the customers are paying money to do the manufacturing process themselves. You know those foam balls, the ones we sell for ninety-nine cents, the one the size of a baseball?

WILL: Yeah.

LEROY: Those things cost less than a penny to make.

WILL: Is that right?

LEROY: That's right.

WILL: Wow. Highway robbery.

LEROY: What?

WILL: Oh, I just—that's a big markup.

LEROY: You think it's dishonest?

WILL: Oh, I—I didn't mean that—

LEROY: You didn't?

WILL: No, I was just . . . It was just a joke.

(They stare at one another. Silence apart from the clunking microwave.)

LEROY: I'm deliberately making you uncomfortable.

(Awkward pause. Will turns off the microwave and takes out his lunch. He sits at a table across the room from Leroy and begins to eat.

Leroy grabs his newspaper and sits down next to Will.)

(Extending a hand) Leroy.

WILL: Oh, it's—

LEROY: Will. I know.

WILL: How do you know my—?

(Leroy points to his nametag.)

Oh. Heh. *(Pointing to Leroy's shirt)* So do you—? You actually wear that to work?

LEROY: For as long as I can before Pauline sees me.

WILL: You don't get in trouble?

LEROY: I'm the only one in this store who knows anything
about art supplies, so I can basically do whatever I want.
I'm the only one that can answer actual questions.

WILL: Are you an artist?

LEROY: Getting my master's in Fine Arts at BSU.

WILL: What kind of art do you make?

(Leroy points to his T-shirt. Pause.)

Oh, sure.

LEROY: I also have one that says "CUNT," one that says,
"YOU WILL EAT YOUR CHILDREN," and one that
has a color photograph of my penis on both sides.

WILL: Oh sure.

LEROY: I'm forcing people to confront words and images they
normally avoid. Especially at a place like this.

WILL: You—you mean the Hobby Lobby?

LEROY: Exactly. It's about the interaction between the word
and the kinds of people who shop here, deliberately making them uncomfortable. Soccer moms and grade-school
kids and little old ladies, they all have to confront the
reality of the words before they get their arts-and-crafts
supplies. You want a foam ball? FUCK. You want some
acrylic paints? CUNT. You want some pipe cleaners?
YOU WILL EAT YOUR CHILDREN. It's the only
reason I work here, I could have got some boring job on
campus just as easy. But where's the art in that?

(Pause.)

WILL: Well, I'm just gonna finish up my—

LEROY: You just move to town?

WILL: Um. Yes, actually.

LEROY: Where from?

WILL: Up north.

LEROY: Where up north?

WILL: Outside of Coeur d'Alene.

LEROY: Where outside of Coeur d'Alene?

WILL: Um. Small town.

LEROY: Beautiful up there.

WILL: Yes, it is, it's really— Have you spent time up there?

LEROY: Little bit. Family trips, you know. Things like that. Kootenai County, right?

WILL: That's right.

LEROY: Rathdrum—that's around there, isn't it?

(Pause.)

WILL: Yeah, that's actually—well, I grew up in Rathdrum.

LEROY: Is that right? Pretty small town, right?

WILL: Pretty small.

LEROY: Must be hard to be in Boise after such a nice little quiet town like that, huh?

WILL: Boise's actually / very nice—

LEROY: What was the name of that church up in Rathdrum? The one that was in the papers a few months ago—Life Church, New Order—?

WILL: New Life Fellowship.

LEROY: Right, New Life. I kind of lost track of the story after a while—is your pastor in jail yet, or is he still awaiting trial? *(Pause)* You see this? This is me deliberately making you uncomfortable. This is your "FUCK" T-shirt.

(Pause.)

WILL: Well, I figured this would happen.

LEROY: I actually think this is kind of cool, it's like I'm talking to a survivor of Jonestown or something.

WILL: Is there a reason that you're doing this?

LEROY: Alex is my little brother. Adopted brother, whatever.

(Pause.)

WILL: I know how this looks. And you're right to be upset but— honestly, after what happened, I'm just trying to start again.

LEROY: You still believe in all that?

WILL: I still believe in God.

LEROY: What about the other stuff? All that crazy Armageddon crap your pastor was preaching about, you still believe in all that?

(Pause.)

WILL: I don't know. *(Pause)* I'm trying to leave all that behind.

(Pause.)

LEROY: Okay, look. I read through some of the articles last night. From what I can tell, you didn't have anything to do with—what happened. And I get that you coming down here is just your ham-fisted attempt to put your life on a new track. But you're going about this in the creepiest way possible, confronting him at work like this.

WILL: I didn't know what else to do. I was worried your parents wouldn't allow me to see him—

LEROY: Yeah, well, John and Cindy drink enough nowadays that they probably wouldn't even care that you're here.

WILL: They—? John and Cindy—?

LEROY: I guess when you handed him off to someone in my parents' church you thought that you were handing him off to good Christian folk, right?

WILL: I didn't have anything to do with his adoption, it was his grandparents / who—

LEROY: Look, I know you came down here to play long lost father, fine, but if you try to "convert" him or whatever—

WILL: I won't. I don't do that anymore.

(Pauline enters with her clipboard, Will and Leroy stop. She senses the tension in the room.)

PAULINE: What?

LEROY: Nothing.

PAULINE: You making enemies already, Leroy?

LEROY: No—

PAULINE: Well, you better not, because the last thing I want to deal with today is fucking conflict resolution and I— *(Noticing Leroy's shirt)* LEROY TAKE THAT FUCKING SHIRT OFF.

LEROY: I didn't bring another one.

PAULINE: I CARE?!

(Leroy takes the shirt off, putting his Hobby Lobby vest on over his bare torso.)

Get out there, you're ten minutes late.

LEROY: Fuck you.

PAULINE: Fuck *you.*

(Leroy exits.)

Fucking hell I wish I could fire that self-righteous little—

LEROY *(Offstage)*: FUCK YOU.

PAULINE: FUCK YOU. *(To Will)* You didn't completely fill out your contact sheet.

WILL: What?

PAULINE: Emergency contact.

WILL: Oh. Um.

PAULINE: Anybody. Family, friend, girlfriend, whatever. Doesn't have to be local.

WILL: I don't really . . .

PAULINE: No *family*?

WILL: Not that I can . . .

(Pause.)

PAULINE: It's for corporate. Gotta put something. Make up a name, I guess.

WILL: Okay.

(Pauline exits. Will fills out the form.)

Scene 6

The next morning. Alex sits at a break room table, reviewing a spool of receipt tape from a register. Two other spools sit in front of him.
    Hobby Lobby TV plays on the TV.
    Will enters, stopping when he sees Alex. Alex looks at him. Awkward silence.

WILL: What's this?

    (No response. Alex continues looking through the receipt tape.)

Sorry.

PAULINE *(Over the PA)*: Mandy to front lines, please. Mandy, front lines.

    (Will goes to a locker, taking out his vest and putting it on. He is about to exit when:)

ALEX: Error in my register countdown yesterday.

(Will turns around.)

WILL: Oh. How much?

ALEX: A hundred and sixty-seven dollars short.

WILL: Ouch.

ALEX: I've never been more than a dollar off. *(Pause)* Pauline wants me to look at the receipt logs for the entire day to see if I can figure out where I made the mistake. I don't even know what I'm looking for.

(Pause.)

WILL: Do you want me to—? *(Pause)* I've done this a hundred times. When I was working at Albertsons I was off all the time.

(Pause. Alex slides one of the receipt spools toward the seat across from him. Will moves to the table and sits down. Will opens up the receipt tape and starts to read it at an extremely fast pace.)

ALEX: Are you really reading it?

WILL: I told you, I've done it a hundred times. My countdowns were always terrible. Trick is to look for too many zeros on the cash tenders. You can skip all the credits and debits.

(Silence as they examine the receipt tape.)

ALEX: They called me this morning.

WILL: The blood test? *(Pause)* Do you believe me now?

ALEX: It doesn't change anything.

WILL: Okay.

(They continue to look.)

Is there anything you'd like to know?

ALEX: Like what?

WILL: About me, about—why you were put up for adoption—

(Anna enters holding the book from before. She smiles at Will, Will smiles back. Anna sits down at a table.)

ALEX: John and Cindy said my real parents were neo-Nazis.

WILL: That's not . . . Um.

ALEX: Well, that's what they said. They said my parents were a couple of neo-Nazis. Are you a neo-Nazi?

(Anna looks up from her book.)

WILL: No, I—

ALEX: Actually, the story about you has changed a few times. When I was little, they told me that you both died in a car accident. Then later, it was that you were neo-Nazis. Then, they said that you beat me.

WILL *(Reading the receipt tape)*: Maybe we should talk about this somewhere else.

(Alex looks at Anna.)

ALEX: Hi, Anna.

ANNA: Um.

ALEX: This is my father. His name is—

(Alex looks at Will's nametag.)

Will. He put me up for adoption when I was a baby, and according to my parents he's a child-beating neo-Nazi who's dead.

*(Anna closes her book and exits quickly.
Silence.)*

WILL: Found it.
ALEX: What?

(Will shows him the receipt tape.)

WILL: See? It's a cash tendered. You entered two hundred instead of twenty.

(Pause.)

ALEX: I've never made a mistake like that before.

(Alex takes the receipt tape from him, circling the mistake.)

(Not looking at him) Thank you.

(Pause. Alex puts down the receipt tape, staring at his hands.)

Okay, I want you to start talking. You'll start talking, you'll tell me things about yourself but when you say something I don't want to hear or don't care about, I'm going to say stop, and you're going to stop, and then say something different.

(Alex reaches into his backpack and takes out a large notebook and a pen. He opens to a page about a quarter of the way through and starts writing.)

WILL: What's—?
ALEX: Stop.

(Pause. Alex continues to write.)

WILL: You were born in a hospital in Coeur / d'Alene—
ALEX: Stop.

(Pause.)

WILL: Your mother and I / were—
ALEX: Stop. I said things about you. Go.

(Pause.)

WILL: I grew up in Rathdrum. My parents were from there, too. It's a little town, about six thousand people. There's a little grocery store that my grandfather started, and my father ran it after he died, but it closed when—
ALEX: Stop. Boring.

(Pause.)

WILL: I'm thirty-nine years / old—
ALEX: Stop.

(Pause.)

WILL: I didn't have anything to do with you being put up for / adoption—
ALEX: Stop.
WILL: Your mother left me after you / were born and she—
ALEX: Stop stop STOP. If you don't stop I'm going to kill myself.

(Alex's breathing speeds up a bit. Long pause.)

WILL: Okay, I— . . . I'm allergic to tuna, but it's not a terrible allergy so I eat it sometimes.

(Alex begins to calm down.)

I don't own any decent pants and I don't know why. I don't like movies.

ALEX (*Still concentrating on his writing*): Why?
WILL: Because they're too violent.
ALEX: There's violence in the world.
WILL: But we don't need to take pleasure in it.
ALEX: That's a stupid thing to say.

(*Pauline appears in the doorway.*)

PAULINE: MANDY? You guys seen Mandy?
ALEX: No.
PAULINE: Fuckin' Mandy.

(*Pauline exits. Pause.*)

WILL: There are things I regret.

(*Alex stops, looks up at him momentarily, then continues writing.*)

More than regret. There are things that tear into me. Things that that make me physically ill.
ALEX: Stop. I don't care how you feel. (*Pause*) Why were you hiding in the scrapbooking section at closing the other day?

(*Pause.*)

WILL: You saw me?
ALEX: Yes.

(*Pause.*)

WILL: I just—needed a quiet place to do some work.
ALEX: What work?
WILL: I'd really rather not—
ALEX: Tell me.
WILL: Alex—

ALEX: *Tell me or I'm gonna kill myself.*
WILL: Why do you say that? You don't really mean that, do you?
ALEX: STOP.

(Pause.)

WILL: It's like—a blog. It's sort of a novel that I'm writing online.
ALEX: People read it?
WILL: Yeah.
ALEX: How many?
WILL: Quite a few. I don't know.
ALEX: What's it about?

(No response.)

What's it about?
WILL: The Rapture.

(Alex stops writing, looks at Will. Pause.)

You actually know what that is?

(Leroy enters.)

ALEX: GO AWAY LEROY I'M DOING SOMETHING.

(Leroy exits, glaring at Will.)

WILL: Do you want to be a composer?

(Alex considers for a second.)

ALEX: Yeah. Kind of.
WILL: What instrument?
ALEX: It's not like that, it's like—performance art. *(Pause)* You
wouldn't understand.

will: No, but I'd like to.

pauline *(Over the PA)*: Will to register four, please. Will, register four.

will: Could you—could I hear some of it sometime? Do you have any recordings of your music, or—?

alex: People don't take me seriously. You wouldn't take me seriously.

will: I would. I take you seriously.

(Alex considers for a moment, then takes his iPod and some iPod speakers out of his backpack.)

alex: Don't look at me.

will: Don't—?

alex: When I'm performing. Don't look at me.

will: Oh, you're going to—?

alex: My music isn't meant to be recorded.

will: You want to—here, right now?

alex: Yeah. Don't look at me.

will: Oh—uh, okay.

(Will turns away from Alex. Alex turns off the TV, then searches around on his iPod for a second. He flips around in his notebook a bit, stopping at a page. He hits play on his iPod. A simple, electronic riff starts to play.)

alex: I got this from a Casio keyboard made in 1989.

will: It's pretty.

alex: *It's not supposed to be pretty.*

will: Okay, I'm sorry. Sorry.

(Alex takes a breath. After a moment, he starts to read. It shouldn't be "singing" per se—but he obviously has very specific ideas on volume, tone, rhythm, etc., that make the reading sound vaguely musical.)

ALEX:

FEED YOUR USELESENESS
FEED YOUR USELESSNESS
CLOWN OF CLOWNS
NATION OF TEARS
I AM HUNGRY
I AM HUNGRY
CLOWN OF CLOWNS
NATION OF TEARS
I AM HUNGRY
I AM HUNGRY
(ants and bedbugs)
(ants and bedbugs)
BLOOD AND GUTS AND FLESH AND TRUTH
BLOOD AND GUTS AND FLESH AND LIES
CLOWN OF CLOWNS
NATION OF TEARS
(ants and bedbugs)
(ants and bedbugs)
I'M EATING TOO FAST
WE'RE EATING TOO FAST
WE'RE CHOKING
CHOKING
CHOKING
CHOKING
SWALLOW IT
CAPITALISM
END

(The song ends abruptly. Alex turns off the music right at the last word. Long pause. Alex looks at Will.)

You can look at me now.

(Will looks at Alex, not knowing what to say. He smiles, claps halfheartedly.)

It's deliberately ironic, it's a statement about consumerism, and— *(Pause)* Fuck this, you don't get it. No one gets it.

WILL: No, it was . . . Thank you. Thank you for doing that for me, that was—neat, it was—really interesting—

ALEX: *Interesting?* I'm gonna kill myself.

PAULINE *(Over the PA)*: Will. Register four. *Now.*

(Alex gets up.)

ALEX: I'm going back to the floor now.

WILL: Wait—

(Will blocks him from leaving.)

ALEX: What are you doing? Stop.

WILL: Please, just—I just want to talk to you—

ALEX: Stop.

(Alex's breathing becomes quicker.)

WILL: I just want to get to / know you—

ALEX: STOP. STOP.

WILL: I'm your father! / I just want to—

ALEX: STOP STOP STOP STOP.

(Alex, becoming more and more agitated, stands up, hyperventilating. He grabs his chest.)

WILL: Okay, I'm sorry—what's the matter? Okay, just—calm down, you're okay—

(Will wraps his arms around Alex. Pauline enters. She sees Alex.)

PAULINE: Fuck me. What did you say to him?

144

WILL: Nothing! I didn't say anything!

(Pauline rushes to the phone, paging over the PA.)

PAULINE: Leroy, break room now.

(Alex gets worse and worse.)

WILL: Alex, just take a breath. Take a breath, / you just need to breathe—
PAULINE: Leroy knows what to do, just get away from him.
WILL: Alex, it's all right. / Just calm down.
PAULINE: Goddammit, Will, I said leave him alone!

(Leroy enters. Will still has Alex in his arms, Alex struggles a bit but Will holds onto him.)

LEROY: GET OFF HIM.

(Will backs off of Alex. Alex slumps down to the floor, Leroy goes to him.)

Okay, buddy, you ready? Look right in my eyes.

(Alex looks at him. They stare at one another silently for a very long time—finally, Alex starts to shake a little less. Very slowly, his breathing starts to regulate. Finally, Alex stops shaking and breathes normally, still looking straight at Leroy.)

ALEX: Chagall?
LEROY: Nope. Kandinsky.
ALEX: It never works.
LEROY: One day.

(Pause. Leroy helps him up.)

PAULINE: Alex, take the rest of the day off, okay?
LEROY *(To Alex)*: You okay?
ALEX: Yeah.
LEROY: I'll drive you home—
ALEX: I have my bike. I'm fine.
PAULINE: You sure?

(Alex gathers his things.)

ALEX: Yeah. *(Pause)* Sorry.
PAULINE: Nothing to be sorry for.

(Alex exits, followed by Leroy.)

I hate it when he does that thing. He'll be fine. But if it happens again, don't go near him, just get Leroy in here as fast as you can, okay?
WILL: Okay.
PAULINE *(Checking her clipboard)*: All right. Well, now we're sort of fucked, we only have two on front lines, and we've got that whole back-to-school display to—

(Leroy reenters, going to Will.)

LEROY: I told you to stay / away from him.
WILL: Leroy, honestly, / I don't know what happened—
PAULINE: Leroy—

(Leroy gets in Will's face, shoving him into the lockers.)

LEROY: WHAT DID YOU SAY TO HIM?

(Pauline rushes over to them, breaking them up.)

PAULINE: OKAY OKAY OKAY ENOUGH.

146

(Leroy moves away from Will. Pause.)

Both of you sit down. Now.

(Will and Leroy sit. Pauline turns off the TV and pulls out a conflict resolution form. She begins to fill it out.)

Fucking conflict resolution, I don't have time for fucking conflict resolution today.

LEROY: Do we have to do this, Pauline?

PAULINE: Fuck you, Leroy. Last year when that guy, what's his name, lazy eye, CARL—when Carl made Mandy cry and Mandy went to corporate and I had to do a *fucking weekend workshop*, so yes, we have to do this. All right. Let's just do this as fast as possible. Each of you, state your case or whatever. Leroy you go first.

LEROY: Sure.

WILL: I didn't mean to—

PAULINE: No interrupting. Leroy, go.

WILL: I really don't feel comfortable with—

PAULINE: FUCK YOU, WILL. Leroy, go. And try to avoid phrasing things in terms of how you feel.

LEROY: I feel this is stupid.

PAULINE: I FEEL FUCK YOU, LEROY.

LEROY: Pauline, do you know who this guy really is?

(Pause.)

PAULINE: What?

LEROY: He's from that crazy end-times church up outside of Coeur d'Alene, in Rathdrum? The one from a few months ago?

(Pause.)

PAULINE *(To Will)*: You're in that church?

will: New Life Fellowship doesn't even exist anymore. I was just a member of the congregation—

leroy: You were like the second in command, you *lived* at the church—

will: No, see, this is something the papers all got wrong. I lived at the church because they paid me to be their bookkeeper and janitor. There were over ninety people in the congregation, I was just one of them. *(Pause)* Pastor Rick is going to jail, and he has to live with the reality of what he did, and I—. . . I was questioned for *months*. I had nothing to do with it.

(Silence. Pauline crumples up the conflict resolution form. She paces a bit.)

pauline: Why the fuck am I always the last one to know what's going on in this store?

leroy: Alex is his son. That he abandoned when Alex was a baby.

(Pauline drops her clipboard, exasperated. Silence. After a few moments, Pauline collects herself.)

pauline: Leroy, clock out and go home.

leroy: *Me?*

pauline: Leroy.

(Leroy angrily grabs his bag out of a locker and leaves the room. Pauline stares at Will.)

will: I didn't mean to cause trouble.

pauline: Be quiet. *(Pause)* You know I can just fire you.

will: I'm a good employee. I don't have a criminal record. You can't fire me because of a church I used to go to.

(Pause.)

PAULINE: I'm gonna say this once, and I hope you understand me. *(Pause)* I took over this store four years ago. The first day I was here, four out of six cashiers called in sick, there were rats in the stockroom, and a good quarter of all items on the floor were mis-stocked or mislabeled. The manager before me, this little pip-squeak from Nampa, he saw there was a mold problem in the air ducts so his solution was to puncture an air freshener and toss it inside. It was *chaos*, you understand? Corporate told me I was taking over as a *temporary* measure, to oversee the branch for six months before, they said, they would most likely close it completely. And what did I do? I cleaned it up. I stayed here during nights by myself restocking and organizing, cleaning the air ducts, firing and hiring, and basically reshaping this entire store from the ground up. I took out ads in the paper announcing new management and grand-reopening sales. Six months later, our profits were up sixty-two percent, and they've been climbing ever since. I, Will, *I* brought order to chaos.

WILL: That's really—impressive.

PAULINE: Goddamn right it's impressive. Damn near *miraculous*. And it happened because of me. Because I changed *everything* about this store, I changed the way this store feels, the way it thinks, the fucking *ecosystem* in this store. And I will not have you or anyone else disrupting the ecosystem I have painstakingly crafted. *(Pause)* Listen, personally, I don't give a shit what you believe. But as far as the good people of Boise are concerned, you are a state-wide embarrassment. And if people were to find out that one of our cashiers is from this wacky little cult up north, they may think about buying their silk flowers somewhere else. *(Pause)* When you're in this store, just—stay away from Alex, understand? And I don't want anyone else finding out about this church of yours. No customers, no co-workers, no one.

(Pauline goes to the TV, turns it on. Hobby Lobby TV resumes.)

You're on register four.

(Will gets up and starts to exit.)

So you still believe in God?

(Pause. Will turns back to Pauline.)

WILL: Yes.
PAULINE: After all that?
WILL: Yes.
PAULINE: Why?

(Pause.)

WILL: You'll see.

(Will exits.)

Scene 7

That night. Will sits in the break room, his laptop hooked up to the ethernet jack on the wall. A blurry close-up of surgery plays on the TV.

Anna enters, seeing Will. She averts her eyes a bit, but doesn't leave. Long pause.

WILL: I can go.

ANNA: It's fine.

(Short pause, then Anna sits down at a table. She notices the TV.)

Oh my God. What is that?

WILL: Oh—I don't know, looks like—I don't even know.

ANNA: That's just disgusting.

WILL: You want me to turn it off?

ANNA: Yes. No. Yes. No, leave it on. Oh my God! Every time I come in here and it's playing these medical things—I just can't stop looking, you know? Oh my God, that's disgusting.

(Pause. Anna smiles a bit at Will, then opens her book.)

WILL: Where were you hiding tonight?

ANNA: Textiles.

WILL: You were?

ANNA: Yes.

WILL: I was there, too.

ANNA: You were not!

WILL: I was, I was next to the back-to-school display, behind the school desk and the—

ANNA: Shut up.

WILL: What?

ANNA: Shut up!

WILL: I'm—what?

ANNA: I was right next to you!

WILL: You were?

ANNA: I was crouched behind the button kiosk! We were five feet away from each other!

WILL: Oh, wow.

ANNA: That's just creepy! Well, that's just creepy. How did we not see each other?

WILL: I'm pretty quiet.

ANNA: So am I. Jesus, it's just so—!

WILL: Please don't— . . . Sorry.

ANNA: What?

WILL: It's just—I'm sorry, the swearing—it's . . .

ANNA: Oh. I'm so sorry.

WILL: It's fine—

ANNA: Sorry.

(Anna almost goes back to reading, then:)

I just want to say I think it's really great that you're here to reconnect with your son, I think that's a great thing to do. I think that's very mature, and very sweet.

WILL: Thank you.

ANNA: I mean, uprooting yourself and moving here from—where are you from?

(Pause.)

WILL: Up north.

ANNA: Up north, you move here from up north and you want to get to know your son, you want to reunite? That's just great, it's really sweet.

WILL: Thank you.

(Pause.)

ANNA: I'm sorry for swearing.

WILL: It's completely fine.

ANNA: It's such a bad habit. Working around Pauline, I think that's what does it. I start to sound like her.

WILL: You don't sound like her.

ANNA: I mean, I grew up Lutheran, my mother's very religious. And I go to church sometimes with her, I have respect for . . . You know, God, and everything. And like I said, I believe in Jesus. *(Pause)* Do you go to a church here?

(Pause.)

WILL: I had a church up north, but I haven't really . . . I haven't found one here yet.

ANNA: Go to the Lutheran church!

WILL: Oh.

ANNA: We do bake sales! We have a bake sale this weekend, you should come!

WILL: Oh, I—

ANNA: And the services aren't ever more than an hour or so, so it's not that bad.

(Will is silent. An awkward moment.)

Oh—I don't mean to be forward.

WILL: No, it's fine, it's not—. I'm not sure if the Lutheran church is for me.

ANNA: Oh yeah, well you gotta, you know. Put thought into that sort of thing. Like buying a new car.

WILL: Sure.

ANNA: "Buying a new car," listen to me. Shut up, Anna. I'm gonna leave you alone to work.

WILL: No, it's . . . I enjoy talking to you.

(Anna blushes.)

ANNA: Oh, shut up, you shut up! You're cute.

WILL: And we both hid in textiles tonight, maybe we're kindred spirits.

ANNA: Oh, shut up!

(Anna hits him with her book, maybe a little too hard.)

Holy shit, I'm sorry.

WILL: It's okay.

ANNA: And I just swore!

WILL: Yes, you did.

ANNA: I'm just sort of an idiot.

WILL: No you're not.

ANNA: I really am, believe me. I think Pauline's ready to fire me.

WILL: Why?

ANNA: Oh, I just don't do anything right. I put the wrong barcode on an entire palette of doll heads the other day, do you believe that? I put the arm and leg barcode on every last one of them. Pauline says I cost the company over a hundred dollars.

WILL: You just made a mistake.

ANNA: Yeah, well, that's one thing I'm good at. I don't even want to tell you how many places I've been fired from in this city. Barnes & Noble, J.C. Penney, three McDonald's, two Wendy's, the Super Walmart and the regular Walmart—pretty soon I'm gonna run out. Have to go back to telemarketing, I really hate telemarketing.

WILL: Are you married? *(Pause)* Sorry, what a dumb thing to just blurt out like that, I just—

ANNA: No, I'm not . . . I have a boyfriend. Well, sort of, we— you know, we date.

WILL: What does he do?

ANNA: He's a telemarketer. *(Quick pause)* And you're a writer!

WILL: Not—really.

ANNA: Well, you write things and people read them, that makes you a writer, doesn't it? Like I said, it's probably better than this book here. I have to stick with it till it's done, but it's just so awful. It's called *Falling from Grace*. You ever read it?

WILL: No.

ANNA: The main character's called "Grace," get it?

WILL: Oh, sure.

ANNA: She lives on this big estate in California, and she has this really rich husband, but all of a sudden he dies in this big car wreck, and turns out that— I'm sorry, what am I doing?

WILL: No, no—keep going.

ANNA: Well, she has to figure out how to live now that she doesn't have this rich husband, and turns out he had all this debt, so she didn't get any money, and then she has to move into this studio apartment and it's hard and blah blah blah. Anyhoo! She's working as a checkout girl, and she falls in love with a customer, and they end up together, and she's happy. And now I'm fifteen pages from the end, so I'm hoping she dies.

(Pause.)

WILL: Wait, I'm sorry, you hope she—?

ANNA: Well c'mon! Why the heck have I read a hundred and eighty pages? To hear about this woman getting married and being *happy*? This is what I'm reading?! I heard once about that book called *Anna*—something. *Anna Karenia?* Is that it? Anyway it's this old Russian novel, someone told me she kills herself at the end and that sounded good but it just looked so long. *(Pause)* Does anyone die in your book?

WILL: Well, it's—about the end of the world, actually.

ANNA: Oh my gosh, a lot of people die then!

WILL: Yeah, quite a few.

ANNA: That sounds so good!

WILL: Thank you.

ANNA: Read some to me! Is that okay that I said that? I'm sorry.

WILL: Oh, well—it's online, you can just—

ANNA: Oh, we don't have a computer at the house. Well, we do, but my dad is the only one who uses it, he doesn't . . . *(Pause)* If you don't wanna read it to me, that's fine. I'm being annoying.

WILL: No, you're not, it's me—I just sort of feel like I've lost faith in what I'm writing.

ANNA: Oh, well, all writers hate their own writing, isn't that a thing?

WILL: Yeah, well. Okay, I can . . . *(Scrolling on the laptop screen)* This is funny, I'm a little nervous.

ANNA: You're nervous because of me?

WILL: A little.

ANNA: Oh, shut up. That's so cute! I'm sorry, that's just so cute, shut up.

(Pause.)

WILL: Okay. *(Reading)* "When Andy woke up that morning to his screeching alarm clock, he knew that something was different. The bedroom in his small apartment was windowless but the darkness he woke up to that morning felt more profound, more deliberate. And as he stumbled his way to the light switch, his forehead sweating, somehow he knew something greater was happening. The light switch didn't work. He opened his bedroom door and squinted his eyes, expecting to be greeted by the same blast of sunshine that hit his face every morning, but felt nothing, and saw nothing." *(Stops)*

Wow this is just terrible, isn't it? It sounds terrible when I read it out loud.

ANNA: No, it's not at all! Keep going!

WILL *(Reading)*: "His living room was pitch black as well. He fumbled through the darkness, barely able to make out the shape of the front door. 'It must still be night,' he thought to himself. 'Something must be wrong with my clock.' He managed to open the front door, and looking outside, he saw—nothing. No sun, no moon, no stars. A blackness had overtaken everything. On a usual morning, Andy would open his door to the street and the McDonald's and the Home Depot he lived next to. But today, there was no traffic. There were no billboards and neon signs. The whole buzz to the world had been taken away, apart from the faint sound of thousands upon thousands of people wandering the streets of the entire suburb, begging for light, cursing Heaven, chewing their tongues, and at that moment Andy lifted his eyes to God and whispered an unconscious prayer of confusion, relief and optimism."

(Long pause.)

ANNA: Holy crap. You really wrote that?

WILL: Yeah.

ANNA: That was so good!

WILL: It sounds so terrible to read it out loud—

ANNA: That totally sounds like a real book, Will! That *is* a real book!

WILL: Thank you.

ANNA: I just . . . WOW! *(Staring at Will)* What are you doing working at a place like this? Why don't you get it published, make some money?

WILL: Oh, it's—sort of complicated—

ANNA: Do you need an agent for that / kind of thing?

WILL: I never really did this / for money—

ANNA: I guess I don't know how all of this works. But you could get an agent, / it's so good.

WILL: It wasn't about that—

ANNA: Oh, sure. You just love writing, / you're an artist.

WILL: I did it because I wanted to spread God's word.

(Pause.)

ANNA: Huh?

WILL: Nothing, never mind.

(Pause. Anna tenses up.)

ANNA: So what kind of church did you go to?

(Pause.)

WILL: I'd actually rather not talk about it—

ANNA: Yeah but what kind of church was it?

WILL: It was a nondenominational—

ANNA: No, I mean like Methodist, Lutheran, whatever—

WILL: That's what I'm saying, it was nondenominational. / Never mind, it doesn't—

ANNA: I don't know what that means.

WILL: It means that we weren't part of any huge network or organization, we just wanted a church that was dedicated to saving people through Christ.

(Pause.)

ANNA: I'm Lutheran.
WILL: Oh.
ANNA: Yeah. I only go sometimes. *(Pause)* You don't know me.

(Pause.)

WILL: What?
ANNA: I said you don't know me.
WILL: I didn't say that I—
ANNA: You know I've had a lot of co-workers like you, super religious guys who try to get me to go to church with them, these little whattayoucallthem, evangelical churches? I even went a couple times. They'd see me sitting and reading my books or whatever, and they'd think, now there's someone who needs help. But let me tell you, I don't need any help, and these churches? No different from a fucking Hobby Lobby, I'll tell you that much. Everyone wants something. So don't think that you know me.
WILL: I'm really not—I'm sorry. I'm not trying to convert you, believe me.
ANNA: You're not?
WILL: No. Really. I'd rather just—not talk about it.

(Pause.)

ANNA: Well what the hell? I'm not good enough for your church or something?
WILL: No, it's . . . I'm just gonna take off, I think.

(Will closes his laptop, putting it into the case. He stands and is about to exit when:)

159

ANNA: Sorry. It's not you. I know I can turn on a dime like that, I'm sorry. I live with my dad, and all my brothers, they make fun of me, especially when I read so . . . Anyway, I'm not good with people.

(Will goes back and sits next to Anna.)

Just do me a favor, okay? If you see God coming again, if you see him coming in his cloud or whatever and he's about to kill us unbelievers, you let me know, 'cause I'll be down on my hands and knees praying for forgiveness then, okay?

(The TV goes to static for a split second and then starts playing Hobby Lobby TV. They both look at it.)

WILL: I thought someone had to jiggle the satellite dish.
ANNA: Sometimes it just flips back on. *(Pause)* I think I'm gonna go. It's nothing you said, just . . . Do you want to leave together? I'm not saying— Oh, gosh, I didn't mean—
WILL: No, it's fine, I—think I'll just stick around for a while longer.
ANNA: How much sleep do you get?
WILL: Lately, not much.

(Will goes back to his laptop, opening it up. Anna starts to exit.)

ANNA: Maybe one of these nights I could try and read your book. Sometimes I can use the computer after my dad falls asleep.

(They smile at one another. Anna exits. Will looks at his laptop for a few moments, then closes it.
He puts a chair in front of the TV and watches it silently.)

Scene 8

Hours later, the middle of the night, in the parking lot. The noise of the interstate is heard. Alex is waiting in the shadows with his backpack. Will enters.

ALEX: Hi.

WILL *(Startled)*: OH. My— Hi.

ALEX: Hi.

WILL: What are you—?

ALEX: I heard Villa-Lobos, were you playing Villa-Lobos in the break room?

WILL: Yeah.

ALEX: You know I don't even really like Villa-Lobos all that much.

WILL: You don't?

ALEX: Not really. I think it's sort of trite.

WILL: Oh. I . . . I really like it. *(Pause)* How did you know I was—?

ALEX: Anna told me you've been spending your nights here.

(Pause.)

WILL: I'm sorry about earlier today, I didn't mean for you to get upset—
ALEX: I want you to tell me about my mom.

(Pause.)

WILL: Okay, / I—
ALEX: Where is she now?

(Pause.)

WILL: I don't know.
ALEX: Where is she now?
WILL: *I don't know.* She was . . . *(Pause)* She—used to get confused, or . . . Right after you were born she left town. I don't know where she went. I haven't heard from her since. Her parents put you up for adoption.
ALEX: Why didn't you take me?
WILL: I couldn't. We weren't legally married, our pastor didn't believe in it. *(Pause)* I tried to, Alex. I really did.

(Pause. Alex calms down a little, taking a step toward Will.)

ALEX: What was she like?
WILL: She loved you very much, she—
ALEX: Stop. What was she like?

(Pause.)

WILL: She wore purple all the time. She loved the outdoors but she was terrified of heights. She played the guitar, and she wrote music. Just like you.
ALEX: Stop. *(Pause)* I don't write music anymore.
WILL: You don't?

162

ALEX: I had a friend I used to write music with, I wrote all my songs with him. We're not friends anymore.

WILL: Why not?

(No response.)

That song you did for me earlier, you wrote that one with him?

ALEX: Yeah.

WILL: You don't have any songs you wrote by yourself?

ALEX: I don't know. I guess. *(Pause)* They're dumb.

WILL: I'd really love to hear one.

ALEX: I haven't even set any of them to music yet.

WILL: That's fine, just—read something to me. You don't need music.

ALEX: No, they're stupid. They're just stupid things I wrote.

WILL: I don't care. I'd just love to hear you read something to me—

ALEX: Stop. *(Pause)* Tell me what your church was like. Go.

(Pause.)

WILL: You know about—?

ALEX: Leroy said you were in some church. He said you guys called yourselves "evangelicals" but that that's just a code word for cult.

WILL: It wasn't a cult.

ALEX: So what was it?

WILL: It doesn't even exist anymore—

ALEX: Tell me or I'm going home. *(Pause)* Go.

(Pause.)

WILL: In the beginning, it was—amazing. We were all young and ambitious. We would sit around with one another for hours, studying the Bible and talking about our lives—we started a church from the *ground up*, we wanted to create something that was—brand-new. And we did. It was—

ALEX: Stop. *(Pause)* If your church was so amazing, why did that kid die?

(Pause.)

WILL: We don't need to talk about / that—

ALEX: Leroy told me the story, but I want to hear it from you.

WILL: Why?

ALEX: Because if you do, I'll tell you some things about me. *(Pause)* Go.

(Pause.)

WILL: Danny was— . . . We both worked at the same Albertsons. He had just graduated from high school. His parents wanted him to go to school and become a pharmacist, he didn't want to leave the congregation. His parents basically disowned him, so he lived at the church with me.

ALEX: You lived together?

WILL: Yes. He was looking for spiritual guidance—so was I, I guess. We helped each other. *(Pause)* One night, after work, Danny and I were in the Albertsons parking lot, and he told me that he—was questioning his faith. I didn't know what to say to him, so I went to our pastor, and—I told him what Danny had said to me.

ALEX: You told on him. *(Pause)* Then what happened?

WILL: You already know the rest of the story—

ALEX: Tell me what happened next. Go.

(Pause.)

WILL: Pastor Rick took him into the wilderness. He wanted to help Danny gain an understanding of his place in God's universe by—bringing him to a point of physical exhaustion. Rick said God was telling him to do it. *(Pause)* About a week later, Pastor Rick comes back to the church, and he tells me he has Danny in the trunk of his car. He says a day earlier he woke up and Danny was stiff. And blue. And he tried to perform CPR, but it didn't work. Then he started to cry—and I called the police. *(Pause)* Yes, I told on Danny. I told on him and if I would have known that Rick was capable of . . . I pray for forgiveness every night, every night I—

ALEX: I was molested by my sixth grade teacher. *(Pause)* Also, I was raped by my fourth grade teacher.

WILL: What?

ALEX: And my fifth and third and second grade teachers.

WILL: Wait—

ALEX: When I was thirteen I was kidnapped for over a week. I was blindfolded in the trunk of a car, every eight hours they would open it up and feed me and give me water without taking the blindfold off. When I was eight, I was camping with my parents and wandered off, and they found me over a month later, and they still don't know how I survived, and I don't remember any of it. All my life, my parents have told me that I'm not important because I'm not their real kid.

(Pause.)

WILL: What are you doing?

ALEX: The thing about being raped in the fourth grade I told Pauline at my interview. And she hired me. The thing about being kidnapped, I told that to my biology teacher. I got an A this semester. The last one about my parents, I told to Leroy. He's confronted them about it before, they always deny it. But he believes me.

(Pause.)

will: So none of that is true?

alex: Nope.

will: Why did you tell me all that?

alex: Because you told me about Daniel Sharp.

(Pause.)

will: Thank you.

(Pause.)

alex: A while ago my best friend started going to one of those—evangelical churches. He said he didn't need music anymore, he said he was happier than music could ever make him. And I'd ask him to tell me about his church, but he said he couldn't talk to me anymore because I was ruining his relationship with God. He doesn't even look at me now. We're in English together, first period, and every fucking morning he looks *so happy*. *(Pause)* That one's true. I haven't told anyone that, not even Leroy.

(Alex looks at Will, considering for a second. He reaches into his backpack, pulling out his notebook. He flips through a few pages and begins to read, meek and self-conscious:)

> My mind folds into itself
> when you pass me
> like I'm a dead man pretending to be asleep
> like I'm a weed growing into itself
> and you pass by me
> you're passing by me
> just now—
> Ah, we once found ourselves
> spread out onto the wet grass
> in the night.

(Pause) I wrote that one without him.

(Long pause.)

It's stupid, I don't know why I read this to you. It's not like
my other stuff, it's trite and sentimental and stupid and—
WILL: That was overwhelming.

(Pause.)

ALEX: You still believe in God?

(Pause. Will looks away.)

WILL: Yes.
ALEX: A God that let Daniel Sharp die in the forest?
WILL: Yes.
ALEX: Why?

(Pause.)

WILL: Because without God, then all I am is a terrible father
who works at a Hobby Lobby and lives in his car. There
are—greater things in life. There have to be.

(Silence. Alex looks at him.)

Scene 9

The next day. Leroy is in the break room wearing a T-shirt that reads "YOU ARE MEAT" in large block letters. Will enters, sees Leroy. The TV is off.

LEROY: Hey.

(Will doesn't respond, goes to his locker.)

Got a call from Cindy this morning, I guess Alex never came home last night.

WILL: Oh.

(Will puts on his vest, is about to leave.)

LEROY: You know, when I was a kid, I really believed all the stuff my parents believed in. God, Jesus, all of it. And I was *terrified*. I used to have nightmares about being in Hell, being tortured forever, couldn't even die to end the pain.

Eight, nine years old and I was having these dreams. And I *promised* myself I wouldn't let Alex go through that. I took him to art galleries, readings . . . I took him to his first concert when he was nine or ten, this recital thing at the university. And then, last year—I caught him in his room reading a Bible, and it was like—how could he be going back to this shit?

(Alex enters.)

(To Alex) Hey.
ALEX: Hi.

(Alex puts his things in his locker.)

That a new shirt?
LEROY: You like it? I can make you one.
ALEX: It's sort of overdone. The font is too aggressive.
LEROY: Wow. Okay, then.
ALEX: I'm just being honest. You want me to lie? Fine. Leroy, you're amazing. You're fucking Picasso.
LEROY: Mom called, said you didn't come home last night. I covered, I told her you came over to my apartment.
ALEX: I don't care what your mom thinks.

(Alex is about to leave.)

LEROY: So what was it, like a father-son Bible study or something?

(Alex stops.)

Are you going to start screaming about Judgment Day on street corners?
ALEX: Leroy, cut it out.

WILL: We just talked.

LEROY: About what?

ALEX: You know it wasn't his fault.

LEROY: What?

ALEX: That kid, up in Rathdrum. It wasn't his fault.

(Pause.)

LEROY: *Goddammit*, Alex, you know this guy is nuts, right?

ALEX: Would you stop? You have no idea what this is like for me, okay?

LEROY: Oh great, are we doing the poor orphan routine now?

WILL: Okay, Leroy—

ALEX: Maybe he has some interesting things to say, did you ever think about that? No, because you're always right, and people who believe different things than you are just stupid. Maybe I'm *interested.*

(Anna enters, wearing noticeably nicer clothes than before. She starts to put her things into a locker.)

Hi, Anna.

ANNA: Morning.

ALEX: I like that shirt.

ANNA: Oh, thanks! *(Smiling, to Will)* Hey, Will.

WILL: Hi.

ANNA *(Going to Will)*: Watch out for Pauline, she just chewed me out for coming in four minutes late!

LEROY *(To Alex)*: Wait wait, so—what? You wanna get like— baptized, or something?

ALEX: I didn't say that, I—. Would you just leave him alone?!

LEROY: WHY ARE YOU DEFENDING HIM? AM I THE ONLY SANE PERSON LEFT IN THIS STORE? You know what, fuck this, I'm taking care of all this right now.

(Leroy goes to the phone and dials a few numbers, putting himself over the PA.)

LEROY *(Over the PA)*: Attention Hobby Lobby employees and guests. This is just a friendly announcement to let you know that one of our new employees, Will Cronin, was directly involved with the cult / up north—

ALEX: Leroy, stop!

LEROY: —that killed a kid out in the forest. He's an unapologetic religious fanatic, and he believes that soon—

(Pauline enters furiously.)

—Jesus will come again and kill everyone who doesn't share his fucked-up beliefs and—

(Pauline heads straight for the phone, hanging it up with her finger. She stares at Leroy.
Leroy takes off his Hobby Lobby vest, throwing it into a garbage can.)

Fuck this. Alex, come on.

(Alex doesn't move.)

ALEX C'MON.

(Again, Alex doesn't move. Pauline whips out a key chain, and in one swift motion, locks the door.)

Pauline.

(Pauline, desperately containing her rage, paces over to the lockers. Leroy tries the door, it doesn't open.)

Pauline, unlock the / fucking door—

PAULINE: SHUT UP SHUT UP SHUT UP. No one's leaving. No one's quitting, just shut up. I just need to—FUCK. I need to think. I just need to think for a minute. Everyone sit down.

(No one moves.)

EVERYONE SIT DOWN NOW.

(Everyone sits.)

(Nearly frantic) Is it too much to ask that we have a normal fucking workday around here?! Here's a news flash for all of you: *What people believe doesn't fucking matter.* What matters are *real* things. Real things like money, the economy and a country so beautiful that it can support a chain of big-box retail stores that makes all it's money off of selling people quilting supplies and construction paper. *That is what matters. (Pause)* All right, here's what we're / gonna—

ALEX: You all think I'm stupid.

LEROY: We don't / think—

ALEX: You think I'm a child.

PAULINE: Okay, Alex, just / calm down—

ALEX: NONE OF YOU GET IT, NONE OF YOU— . . .
(Pause) In less than a year, I'm gonna graduate. What the hell am I gonna do then?

(Short pause.)

LEROY: After you—? Where is this coming from? You have a plan. You're going to BSU, if the financial aid doesn't come through—

ALEX: That's your plan, not mine. And even if I do that, go to school and major in music, then what? You think I'm gonna like, be the next fucking big thing?

LEROY: Why not?

ALEX *(Increasingly upset)*: Okay, so I make a few albums, do some performances, probably wind up teaching, and that's like the *best-case scenario*. I'll probably just fail completely, come back to Boise, and end up working at this fucking Hobby Lobby—

LEROY: Okay, / calm down—

WILL: Alex, it's / okay—

ALEX *(Losing himself)*: —working at *this fucking store*, for the *rest of my life*. And what's the alternative? Believing in what my dad believes in, believing in some magical guy up in the clouds who created us *for fun* I guess, a guy who is going to come pretty soon to kill us all. These are my two options in life, and they are *fucking meaningless*.

LEROY *(Cold)*: OKAY ALEX.

(Silence.)

PAULINE: Okay, let's all just—. We're all calm, okay? Everybody's calm.

(Pauline paces for a moment, thinking. Finally, she looks at Will.)

All right, there's only one way to deal with this. Will, I'm sorry—you can finish out the rest of your day, but after that you're gonna have to find work somewhere else.

WILL: What exactly am I being / fired for?

PAULINE: *Look around.* One week ago, this store was doing just fine—now it is *chaos*. Alex is my most accurate cashier, Leroy knows more about art supplies than anyone in this entire company. It's either them or you. I will make up a reason for corporate if I have to. *(Pause)* Anna, go out to the floor. Tell any customer you see that a teenager got on the PA or something.

(Pauline unlocks the door.)

ANNA: Oh—uh, I don't—
PAULINE: ANNA, GO NOW.

(Anna exits.)

Will, register three. *(Pause)* Please.

(Pause. Will considers, then finally makes his way back to the floor.)

There's four palettes that need to be stocked.

(Pause.)

LEROY: Yeah, okay.

(Pauline goes to the TV, turns it on. Hobby Lobby TV plays.)

PAULINE: And both of you—do me a favor and stay away from him for the rest of the day. Okay?

(Pauline exits. Silence.
   Leroy gets up and goes to the trash, taking out his vest. He puts it back on.)

LEROY: Look, buddy, just— . . . I wish I could give you some big answer, but the truth is we all just do the best we can. *(Pause)* You ready?

(Silence.)

ALEX: Think of one.

(Pause.)

LEROY: Right now?

ALEX: Yeah.

LEROY: No, Alex, c'mon.

ALEX: I just feel like it, let's just try. C'mon.

(Pause.)

LEROY: Uh. Okay, I got one.

(Leroy looks into Alex's eyes. Silence. Alex stares into his eyes for a long moment.)

ALEX: Pollock.

(Pause.)

LEROY: Nope. It's—

ALEX: DON'T TELL ME. *(Pause)* Rauschenberg.

(Leroy shakes his head.)

Duchamp.

LEROY: No—

ALEX: Frida Kahlo. Andres Serrano. Andy Warhol.

LEROY: Alex, enough. You're not gonna get it. *(Pause)* You wanna keep working, or you wanna go home?

(Silence.)

ALEX: I wanna go home.

LEROY: Okay. Just give me a minute, I'll go talk to Pauline and then I'll take you home, all right?

(Leroy exits. Alex sits motionless for a second, then looks at Hobby Lobby TV. He sits for a long moment listening to the TV, before standing up and turning up the volume.

For the first time the voices are heard clearly. The two men speak very slowly, nearly in a monotone.)

HOBBY LOBBY TV VOICE 1: —and so it's, uh. Yeah, it's I think— what's the retail on this?

HOBBY LOBBY TV VOICE 2: It's, uh—

HOBBY LOBBY TV VOICE 1: It's really a great / product, you know—

HOBBY LOBBY TV VOICE 2: It's ninety-seven.

HOBBY LOBBY TV VOICE 1: What's that?

HOBBY LOBBY TV VOICE 2: Ninety-seven cents. The unit, it's uh. Ninety-seven.

(Slowly, Alex sits down, keeping his eyes on the TV.)

HOBBY LOBBY TV VOICE 1: Oh, see and that's—that's down from last year. That same unit, uhhh . . . That was, I wanna say a dollar ten last year. But we, you know. We talked with our distributor, and he—

HOBBY LOBBY TV VOICE 2: It's always nice when we can offer these savings.

HOBBY LOBBY TV VOICE 1: Yeah, it's. It's good to, you know, point the customers toward savings like these. It's a good thing for our employees to keep in mind. I'll tell you, you know, it's also. It's a good product. It's really—you can really do a lot with something like this. Kids love it, and it's good for kids—they can be so creative with things like this—

HOBBY LOBBY TV VOICE 2: Durable, too.

HOBBY LOBBY TV VOICE 1: Oh, yeah. You know, it's popular during back to school, it's. Teachers, you know, art teachers, they pick these up—school districts, they love these, and it's great / when we—

HOBBY LOBBY TV VOICE 2: This year, for the first time, we've been sending fliers out to individual school districts, and we've been getting a great response. The teachers, uh, appreciate it.

(Alex continues to watch, becoming more and more upset. His breathing becomes quicker.)

This is, uh. Store number 1478 in Cedar Rapids, they sent out some fliers to the local school board, and they said they've seen an increase in sales, uh, a four-percent increase. For the Fall Quarter, four percent. Really good stuff.

HOBBY LOBBY TV VOICE 1: Well, and you know, when you offer quality products like this, uh. You can—feel proud that we can serve our own community by giving them products like these at such low prices.

HOBBY LOBBY TV VOICE 2: And that we're helping these kids in their education—art is so important for these kids to learn at an early age, that's really what. It's something this company, it's founded on that.

(For a moment, it looks like Alex is having another panic attack—but this changes into a quieter, deeper grief.)

HOBBY LOBBY TV VOICE 1: And you wanna give kids the best art supplies without going bankrupt.

HOBBY LOBBY TV VOICE 2: Yeah, exactly. / So this is—

HOBBY LOBBY TV VOICE 1: This is—yep, this is really just a solid product, great for art classes. *(Pause)* Another great product here—you see this?

HOBBY LOBBY TV VOICE 2: Oh yeah.

(Leroy enters.)

hobby lobby tv voice 1: / We had this on the shelves down in store 1089 in Tallahassee—

leroy: She says she'll want you to make up the hours this weekend. Mandy's off. *(Pause)* You ready?

alex: I'll meet you outside.

(Leroy gives up and exits.)

hobby lobby tv voice 1: —and it was off the shelves almost immediately, so we started introducing it nationwide starting last year.

(Alex pulls out his notebook, opens to a page, and begins to write.)

hobby lobby tv voice 2: We've been getting, uh. A really—a good response to the item, especially in our Southeastern Division, Midwest Division—

Scene 10

Much later that night. Will, looking tired and worn out, stares at the TV, which plays an extreme close-up of eye surgery. Alex's notebook is next to him on the table, open to a page.

    Anna enters with a book. She sees Will immediately. Will continues to stare at the TV. Not knowing exactly what to do, Anna sits down at a table at the other side of the room and starts to read.

WILL: What're you doing here so late?

ANNA: Couldn't sleep. I don't live far. Just thought I'd—finish up my book.

WILL: How'd you get in?

ANNA: I stole Pauline's spare key ring this afternoon. Got tired of hiding. I figure if she finds out, who cares, I'll go work somewhere else. This place is kinda boring anyway. *(Looking at the TV)* Oh, gosh, that's an eye, isn't it?

WILL: Yeah. I think so.

(Anna moves over to him and sits with him. Will finally looks at Anna.)

ANNA: I read that book of yours. Story, whatever it is. It's— really good. *(Pause)* Listen, I know what getting fired feels like. I know. But there are plenty of other places in town you can get a job. My friend Ally, she just got a job at the Costco in Eagle, I could call her and—

WILL: I don't care about getting fired.

(Pause.)

ANNA: Oh. *(Pause)* Then what's / the—

WILL: Alex and I talked for hours in the parking lot last night. He promised me he would meet me here again tonight. He was supposed to be here hours ago. *(Picking up Alex's notebook)* He left this in my locker.

(Pause.)

ANNA: What's it / say?

WILL: It says, "Hell is all around us." *(Pause)* I think I might be a bad person.

(Pause. Slowly, Anna wraps her arms around Will in a hug. It's awkward at first, Will is uncomfortable.)

No—

(Anna doesn't let go. Will takes a breath and they both settle into it, holding one another. Silence.)

ANNA: You know what part of your book I liked best?

(Pause.)

WILL: What's that?

(Anna breaks the hug, but they remain close.)

ANNA: There was that part with the pilot—what's his name?
WILL: Mark.
ANNA: Yeah! Mark. And Mark was flying over Israel and suddenly
    he looks out the window and he sees the, uh—the / four—
WILL: Four horsemen of the apocalypse.
ANNA: Yeah, and he knows that the world is gonna end, like,
    soon. And he thinks back on his life, and he realizes all
    of the bad things he's done, all of the sex and drugs and
    lies and whatever, and all he wishes is that he could have
    repented everything in time. But it was too late. And then
    he dies. And no one can help him. *(Pause)* Anyway, that
    was my favorite part.

(Pause.)

WILL: The last time I saw Danny, we hid in the Albertsons
    until everyone had left and then we went out into the
    parking lot, and we prayed for Christ to come again. We
    prayed for all of it to go away, we prayed for all of it to
    be swallowed up in divine fire, every disgusting house
    and parking lot and interstate and car and person on fire
    turning into ash and reforming as a city of pure light that
    was brilliant and eternal and unchanging. And we prayed,
    "Dear Jesus, now."
        . . .
        . . .
        . . .
    Now.
        . . .
        . . .
        . . .

Now.

. . .

. . .

. . .

Now.

. . .

. . .

. . .

And then nothing happened.

(Long silence.)

ANNA: Would you like to go to church with me on Sunday?

(Pause. Will looks at her.)

Look, I don't meet a lot of guys, and the ones I do meet are pretty much terrible. But you come in here at night just like I do, and you're such a talented writer, and I . . . And listen, you're not the only one with a checkered past, okay? When I dropped out of high school, I— . . . Anyway, I don't even need to tell you, let's just say that my father, he has good reason to be the overbearing asshole that he is. But I just think if you could come to church with me, if we could go together . . . The pastor, his name is Edward, but everyone calls him "Pastor Eddie," it's really nice. And it's not all about Hell and sin and whatever, it's just a nice community organization. They're very open-minded, we even have a gay couple that comes to our church, and no one even thinks twice about it. We have a food bank, and a youth group, and— . . . *(Pause)* Will, you can just believe in something else!

WILL: Believe in what? Believe in the Lutheran Church, some branch of some branch of some branch of Christianity, some organization that's going to legislate my belief system instead of looking to God's word for it? You work at a Hobby Lobby, Anna. Your life is meaningless, *my* life is meaningless, and the only thing that gives any meaning, that brings any hope to this life is the fact that God will come again in glory to replace this disgusting life with something new, and pure, and eternal—

ANNA: Okay, Will.

WILL *(Rising)*: And you could take the easy route, you could go to a liberal church, and believe in nothing, believe that God is unknowable and we'll never know the meaning of life. You'll go to college and get a degree in English or philosophy or art or economics and you'll spend your life searching in the dark, trying to find meaning in meaninglessness—become one of those people who sit around in their fashionable clothes with their fashionable friends and call us bigots, and fanatics and hicks, calling us idiots for actually *believing* in something, for *standing* for *truth*—

ANNA: Will, stop!

WILL *(Losing himself)*: AND THESE PEOPLE WILL BURN IN HELL, *YOU* WILL BURN IN HELL BECAUSE INSTEAD OF SEEKING TRUTH YOU MOCK IT, YOU INSULT IT, AND SOON GOD *WILL* COME AND—

(With a quick burst of static, the TV flips back to Hobby Lobby TV. Will stops, looking at the TV. Pause.
  Anna takes her book and quickly exits.
  The scene immediately shifts to:)

Scene 11

Later that same night, in the parking lot. Will stands, bathed in the
fluorescent light, listening to the interstate. Leroy enters behind him.

LEROY: Hey.

> *(Will turns around. Pause.)*

Get in my truck.

> *(Pause.)*

WILL: Why?

LEROY: This afternoon Alex swallowed an entire bottle of my
mom's sleeping pills. He's stable, they pumped his stomach. But the doctors said he should be sent to some kind
of juvenile mental health facility, something like that,
where he won't be a danger to himself.

(Pause. Will is horrified.)

WILL: Why did he—?

LEROY: Only said one thing to me. When I asked him why he did it, he said, "Hell is all around us." *(Pause)* So right now you're going to get in my truck, I'm going to take you to the hospital, and you're going to talk to him. You're going to tell him that there's no Heaven, no Hell, no apocalypse. No God.

(Pause.)

WILL: I'm—I'm sorry—

LEROY: Listen, you can go on believing in this bullshit, or you can give it up right now. You wanna be his dad? Now's your chance. *(Pause)* Well?

(Will, holding back tears, looks away from Leroy. He closes his eyes.)

WILL: Now.

  . . .

  . . .

  . . .

  Now.

LEROY: What are you—?

(Long silence.)

WILL: Now.

(Will doesn't move. Finally, Leroy gives up and exits. Will looks back to the interstate, standing in the wash of fluorescent light. Long pause as he listens.)

Now.

(The sounds of the interstate start to get louder.)

Now.

(The light becomes brighter.)

Now.

(As the light becomes brighter and brighter, the sounds of the interstate grow louder and louder, changing pitch, becoming deeper and more violent.)

Now.

(The light reaches an uncomfortable level of brightness, and the sound of the interstate becomes increasingly more and more distorted.)

Now.

(As the light reaches its brightest point, the sounds of the interstate morph into what sounds like one continuous, monotonous explosion—a low, rumbling, unsettling drone that continues throughout the scene.
Alex enters.)

ALEX: It never works.
WILL: One day.

(Pause.)

ALEX: I was up early this morning, went for a drive up to those mountains outside of town. *(Pause)* I felt like I should pray. So I got out of the car, and I knelt down on the ground, and I wanted to pray but I couldn't pray anything.

WILL: It's okay, Danny, we could pray together before work.

ALEX: No, that's not it, I . . . *(Pause)* When I wake up in the morning, I feel sick. Like I don't want to get out of bed. And then I see you, and you look so happy. You look perfect.

(Pause.)

WILL: I'm not perfect, Danny.

ALEX: Yes. You are. I see you, and you're so perfect, and I'm—. *(Pause)* I think I might be a bad person.

WILL: No, you're not. You're just letting the world get to you. In God's eyes, you're—beautiful. You're perfect.

ALEX: Pastor Rick is trying so hard / with me—

WILL: Danny, one day none of this will matter. When all this is swallowed up. When we become bodies of pure light. Our perfect souls ripped out of these awful bodies and reborn. Both of us. Can you imagine what that will feel like?

(Pause.)

ALEX: Will, I'm not sure I believe in God.

(Long silence.)

Say something. *(Pause)* Will. Say something.

(Long pause.)

I'm going to walk home tonight.

*(Alex exits.
    The lights suddenly return to normal. The drone immediately returns to the normal sounds of the interstate. Will is left alone in the parking lot.*

A car is heard passing on the interstate. Silence. Another car passes.

Will stares forward. Another silence.

He waits.)

END OF PLAY

SAMUEL D. HUNTER's plays include *The Whale* (2013 Drama Desk Award, 2013 Lucille Lortel Award for Outstanding Play, 2013 GLAAD Media Award, Drama League and Outer Critics Circle nominations for Best Play), *A Bright New Boise* (2011 Obie Award for Playwriting, 2011 Drama Desk nomination for Best Play). His latest plays include *The Few*, *A Great Wilderness*, *Rest* and *Pocatello*. His plays have been produced by Playwrights Horizons, Rattlestick Playwrights Theater, Seattle Repertory Theatre, Victory Gardens, South Coast Repertory, Williamstown Theater Festival, The Old Globe, Woolly Mammoth Theatre Company, Denver Center Theatre Company, Clubbed Thumb and Page 73. His work has been developed at the O'Neill Playwrights Conference, the Ojai Playwrights Conference, Seven Devils Playwrights Conference and elsewhere. Sam is the winner of a 2012 Whiting Writers' Award, the 2013 Otis Guernsey New Voices Award, the 2011 Sky Cooper Prize and the 2008–09 PoNY Fellowship. He is a member of New Dramatists, an Ensemble Playwright at Victory Gardens, a Core Member of The Playwrights' Center, a member of Partial Comfort Productions and was a 2013 Resident Playwright at Arena Stage. A native of northern Idaho, Sam lives in New York City. He holds degrees in playwriting from New York University, The Iowa Playwrights Workshop and Juilliard.